BREAKING INTO THE NEW

Object lessons for
young children

by
Alex Russell

MOORLEY'S Print & Publishing

© Copyright 1999

All rights reserved. No part of this publication may be reproduced, stored in a retrieval system, or transmitted, in any form or by any means, electronic, mechanical, photocopying, recording or otherwise, without the prior written permission of the publishers.

British Library Cataloguing in Publication Data.
A catalogue record for this book is available from the British Library.

MOORLEY'S Print & Publishing
23 Park Rd., Ilkeston, Derbys DE7 5DA
Tel/Fax: (0115) 932 0643

ISBN 0 86071 534 5

Dedicated to my grand-children, Kirsten, James and Hannah
that from childhood they may know the scriptures.

I wish to thank Mrs May McNeil for her labour of love
in proof reading the original manuscript
and to Kenneth Drummond for the graphics.

CONTENTS

1. Breaking into the New - First Sunday of Year 5
2. Talk about Nothing 8
3. The Shape of Love - For Valentine's Day 11
4. The World's Takeaway 14
5. Guessing Your Thoughts 17
6. Total Commitment - For the end of a mission 20
7. Strawberries on a plate - For Stewardship Sunday 22
8. God's Ferry Boat 25
9. Faithful in Little Things 28
10. The Five Senses - For very young children 31
11. Den of Robbers or House of Prayer 35
12. Trinity Sunday 38
13. The NO UO Mothers' Day - For Mothers' Day 42
14. The Two Spiders - For Missionary Sunday 45
15. Wholehearted 49
16. Many Happy Returns 52
17. Borrowland - For Palm Sunday 55
18. The 5P Easter - For Easter Sunday 58
19. Missing, but Alive - For Pentecost Sunday 62
20. Bible Leftovers - For Harvest Sunday 66
21. How long will it last? - For All Saints Day 70
22. The Elephant Never Forgets - For Remembrance Sunday 73
23. A Word in Season - For Advent Sunday 76
24. Christmas Cracker - For Christmas Day 80
25. The End- Sad or Glad? - For Last Sunday of Year 84

BREAKING INTO THE NEW

(First Sunday of year)

Material and Preparation
For this talk we need a packet of biscuits or some package that is tightly wrapped and therefore hard to open. I find new Audio cassettes in that category.

It would also be helpful to have four mouths cut out and joined at one end with a paper clip so that they could be spread out as many mouths or brought together as one mouth (see fig. 1 & 2).

Do the same with ears as with the mouth (see fig. 3 & 4).

Have longer strips of card with 'mine' written on one side of the card and 'yours' on the other. Again have these joined at one end with a paper clip (see fig. 5).
Have a card with a sad face on one side and a glad face on the other (see fig. 6 & 7).

There is a text of scripture for each point which you may want up on the O.H.P. or written on card.

Did you know, children, the beginning of a New Year is a time when people say they are going to change their ways. We call these plans New Year resolutions. That just means there are people who have promised themselves that this year 'I will get up earlier for work' or 'I will not be so untidy' or 'I will be more patient'. 'I will watch my language'.

Many people, who make these promises, find them hard to keep. Did any of you promise yourself to change in the New Year?

Here is the reason so many people fail. *(Bring out the packet of biscuits)* Bear with me, boys and girls, I find these packets so hard to open. Have you found that? It is the same with those blank tapes you buy. What a time it takes me to open them!

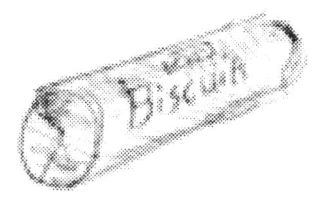

Would someone like to help me open this packet? Looks like you have the same problem I have. And that is the reason we fail to change our ways in a New Year. The Spirit of the Lord finds it hard to break into our lives. We keep Him out. We try to change on our own and in our own strength.

What would happen if the Lord got through the wrapper of our lives and came in to be our Friend? Here are the changes I think would come:
We would

1. Talk less and listen more

We are told 'it is good to talk', and that is true; especially, when things trouble us or people bully us. But there are times when we talk more than we listen. *(Spread out the mouths and leave only one ear showing.)*

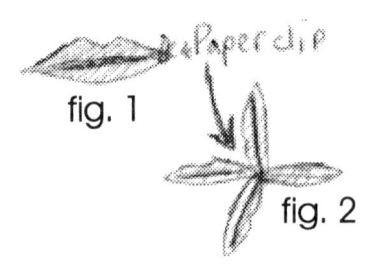

fig. 1

fig. 2

When Jesus becomes our friend, things change. *(Bring the mouths together as one and spread out the ears.)* We talk less and listen more.

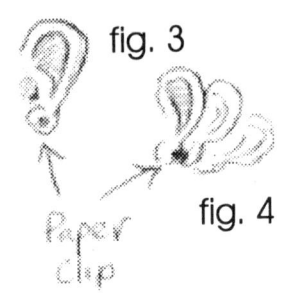

fig. 3

fig. 4

The Bible puts it this way in the book of James. **'Be slow to speak and quick to listen'.** James 1v19.

Let's make this year a good listening year. A wise son or daughter listens to those who know better. Listen to parents and teachers. Have a quiet time so you can listen to God through the Bible reading for the day and before you pray.

Something else would change if we let Jesus through the wrappings. We would:

2. Grab less and give more

How many times do we think to ourselves, 'I want that cake'? 'I'll steal that pen if she won't lend it to me.' 'I will just keep the book I borrowed, he will never ask for it now.'
(Open up the cards with 'mine' on each one and grab them under your arm.)

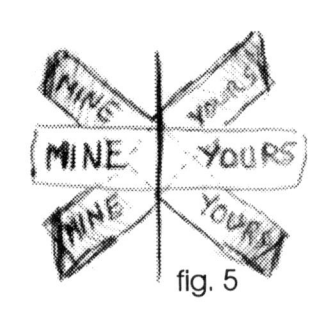

fig. 5

If Jesus has His way something changes.
(Turn the cards over to reveal the word 'Yours' on each of the cards. and have the cards reach out to the children). Do you see what is happening? Instead of 'mine' 'mine' 'mine', it is 'yours', 'yours', 'yours'. We start to open our closed fist and say, 'Do have some cake!' 'Would you share this with me?' 'Oh, by the way, here is the book I borrowed.' 'Lord, here is the money for the offering. I give it back to You.'

Jesus said this, **'It is more blessed to give than to receive.'** Acts 20v35. Let's make this a giving year.

Another change if Jesus broke through into our lives is this:
We would

3. Sulk less and shine more

Do you know what it means to sulk? Yes, it is having a long, coffee-pot face. Not very nice to live with. *(Show your card with the sad face.)*
What a miserable looking face! Here is the good news. Those who know Jesus have a right to be happy. They don't need to live like Mr Grumpy. When the Lord comes in with His light and shows up all the wrong things that need to be put right; when we say sorry to Jesus, then we can light up for Jesus. We can shine for Him. *(Show the glad face on the card)* Doesn't that face look happy?
Jesus said:
Let your light so shine before men, that they may see your good deeds and praise your Father in Heaven. Matthew 5v16.
Let's make this a shine-for-Jesus year.
Can we really sing: 'This little light of mine, I'm gonna let it shine'?

When Jesus comes in and sin goes out, the change in us stays all through the year.

TALK ABOUT NOTHING
Hebrews 13v8

Materials and Preparation
This is a message on the uniqueness of Jesus in a world where He is one among many. It is partly a wordless presentation in that we will use symbols for each point made.
Cut out three large 'O's and three '2's. Also three large mathematical signs:

The three points of this talk will be:
- O 2 + Nothing to add (to Him)
- O 2 - Nothing to take away (from Him)
- O 2 = Nothing to equal (Him)

Use bright card and a black board.

(This talk can be easily adapted to the year 2000)

There is a story told, about the minister who asked the children at his church a question. A boy put up his hand, "Please sir, I don't understand the question but the answer is 'Jesus'."

I wonder how many times you have been asked a question at church and the answer expected is 'Jesus'. Let me try and explain with these signs why Jesus is the answer to so many questions. *(Hold up one of the 'O's)*. If I were to write this number as a word what would it be? Yes, 'nothing'. Let's use that word every time you see an '**O**'.

What is this number? *(Hold up a '2')* Yes, a two. For this talk every time you see a '**2**' we will think of the word 'to'.

Let me see if you know some of the signs you learn at school. What is this one? (Show (+) sign) Yes, this sign means 'plus' or 'add'. We will use 'add'.

What about this one? *(Show (-) sign)* This one could mean 'minus' 'subtract' or 'take away'. We will use 'Take away'. Towns are full of 'take-aways'.

Here is the last one. Any guesses? *(Show (=) sign)* Yes, this means 'equals'. We will say equal.

Here is the first reason Jesus is the answer to so many questions. Let me put the signs on the board. (You could use an O.H.P.) See if you can give me the first part of this talk.

        O   2   +   to Him

Yes, **'nothing to add to Him'**. No matter how many years people have thought about Jesus, there is nothing we can add to him that will make Him more precious than He already is. We, mistakenly, try to add some of our goodness, or some of our effort to make Jesus accept us. But He loved us even when we never gave Him a thought.

Fig. 1

This 'add' sign reminds us of the cross on which He died for all the wrong things we have done. There is no other person we need to know because no one else ever said He was the way, the truth and the life and the only way to God.

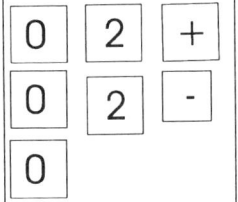

How true, then, there is nothing to add to him. Can you work out the second part of this talk?

        O   2   -   from Him

That's it. **Nothing to take away from Him.** This is the second reason Jesus is the answer to so many questions.

Fig. 2

Some people, over the years, have wanted to take away from Jesus the miracles He did, such as healing the sick or stilling the storm.

Jesus Christ is the same yesterday, today and forever

Hebrews 13v 8

Others have wanted to take away the fact that Jesus always existed as God's Son even, before He came at Bethlehem as a baby. But there is nothing we can take away from Jesus and still have the Jesus we read of in the Bible. *(Show text from Hebrews 13v8.)*

The Bible tells us 'Jesus Christ is the same yesterday, and today and forever.'

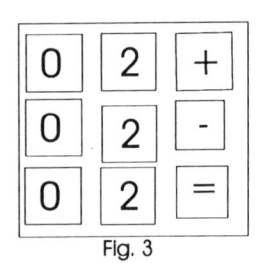

Fig. 3

Here is the third reason Jesus is the answer to so many questions. Can you work this one out?

O   2   =   Him

Yes, **nothing to equal Him**. There are all kinds of people who want us to follow them; pop stars, football stars. Some have even said they are more famous than Jesus Christ. Sadly, many of them disappoint us by the way they live. Others have come to know Jesus as the answer to all their needs. Can you think of any stars who have come to know Jesus?

You see, there is no one to equal Jesus as the Saviour of the world.

This is a talk about 'nothing'.
> **Nothing to add to Him.**
> **Nothing to take away from Him.**
> **Nothing to equal Him.**

THE SHAPE OF LOVE
(For Valentine's Day)
Text John 13v1 '... **Having loved his own who were in the world, He now showed them the full extent of his love.**'

Materials and Preparation
For this talk we need the wheel of a bicycle. It should be in good condition and may have the tyre on or off. There may a slight advantage in having the tyre on the wheel for the end of the talk.

It would be helpful to have one of those small coloured message pads with the sticky edge on which you can write, as you give the talk, the different organisations of the church and you may want to single out some of the names of leaders in the church including the children's work.

Have another of those coloured pads to write four times **HIS LOVE** *and once* **JESUS**. *Hide the wheel until a certain point in the talk.*

This is a special Sunday today, boys and girls. Can anyone tell me what is special about it? Yes, It's St. Valentine's Day. Have any in the church received a card today? Well, that is something, but I need to tell those who have received a card that those of us who didn't, don't need one to tell us how beautiful we are because we know that already. No one need be sad today.

There were actually two St Valentines. One was a priest in Rome who used to give shelter to Christians who were being hunted by those who wanted to torture them. This Valentine became a Christian and is supposed to have restored the sight of a jailer's daughter. He met a violent death about 240 years after Jesus. His day is on the 14th of February.

The other St Valentine was a bishop, who was also put to death for being a Christian a few years later. The feasts of both saints are celebrated on the same day.

Sending Valentines, or love tokens, was a Roman custom on the same day as Valentine's Day, which accidentally brought the two together. It was also said that around that time the mating season of birds began.

Enough of the background. If I were to ask those who received a card what shape love is, they would think I was being silly. "How can love have a shape?" you might say. Well, what shape do you find on the front of most Valentine cards? Yes, a heart. Not a bad idea, when you think that to really love someone you would give them your heart or your all.

I am going to dare to be different today and say that love is round shaped. Of course I am thinking about a very special love, called Christian love or God's love and I believe it is shaped like a circle.

Let me show you. *(Bring out the wheel, which up to this point has been hidden).* I wonder if you can tell me the different parts of a wheel. Yes, that is the rim of the wheel. Yes, those are the spokes of the wheel. And yes, right at the centre is the hub of the wheel. That's all we need to know for today.

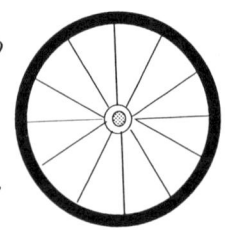

I would like a boy or a girl to come out and do something for me. Could you examine the rim of this wheel and tell where the people who made the rim started it and finished it? Is there a place where two bits have been joined up? You mean you can't find where they join? Do you mean the rim as no beginning and no ending? Well, that's why I want you to think of God's great love for us like a wheel. Do you know the song to the tune of 'Puff the magic dragon'? Let's sing it!

God's love is like a circle, a circle big and round
And when you see a circle no ending can be found,
And so the love of Jesus goes on eternally,
Forever and forever, I know that He loves me.

There it is then; love is like a circle. I am going to write HIS LOVE four times and stick it round the rim so we will remember that God's love for us never ends.

But my wheel is not all rim. It has spokes. I want us to imagine these spokes are all the people in the church. I will just write some of the organisations of the church. Can you tell me what they are? *(Quickly write out organisations and stick them on separate spokes.)* I tell you what, let's put some people on these spokes who help us in the church. There is Mabel who cleans the church; we will put her on. She is our spokesperson for the cupboard. Yes, I'm sure she talks and sings as she cleans. *(Go through whatever names you feel would be appropriate. Some with learning difficulties might appreciate a mention. Call them a spokesman or spokesperson.)* The fact is boys and girls, you are all there, everyone in the church.

That just leaves the hub at the centre. I am going to write the name of someone who deserves a place at the centre of this wheel. Someone who showed His love by dying for us on a Cross. Yes, Jesus! I will stick His name right on the centre of the wheel. Jesus, you know, should always be at the centre of our lives, whether at school or at home or in church.

There is just one more thing I want you to notice. Can you tell me what happens to the spokes, the closer they get to the centre? How close are they? Yes, very close. Up at the rim they are further apart but down there at the rim they are mighty close. Listen to this. The closer we get to Jesus and what He wants for our lives the closer we, as a church, get together or put another way, the more we love each other.

We don't need to send cards to each other one day in the year, but all year we can show our love by caring for each other, praying for each other and being kind to each other.

Just one more point. **Have love will travel.** With His love all around, Jesus at the centre and all you good folks getting closer together there is no telling where such a love will take us. Happy Valentine's Day!

What shape is Christian love? It is round.

THE WORLD'S TAKEAWAY
2 Kings 20 v 13

Materials and Preparation

You will need a purse and a piggy bank or just a jar where money could be kept. A few other items such as tools and jewellery, which looks expensive, would help in telling the following story. Have a thief's bag to put the items into as you tell the story.

*Have three cards with the following: **JOY, PEACE, and LOVE**.*
Study the story of Hezekiah in 2 Kings 20v 12- 19, and link it with John 10 v 10. This story is adapted from an article in the Times by Peter Foster.

I want to tell you a story today, children. It's about a boy called Russell Brown who was four years of age and in 1996, when this story was told, he lived in Alderman's Green, Coventry.

Now young Russell woke up in the middle of the night to go to the bathroom. What he didn't realise was that he had two other friends in the house, who had arrived unexpectedly at the same time as he got up.

Can you guess who these unexpected friends might be? Yes, burglars. How do you think you would feel if you woke up in the middle of the night and found burglars? Yes, frightened.

But young Russell didn't seem to be scared at all. In fact he promised to be a good boy and make no noise while his parents slept upstairs.

The burglars, as his friends, you understand, must have asked him where the money was kept. They were told his mummy kept her purse hidden in the kitchen. It had £200 in it. (*Show purse.*) He also obliged by showing them where there was more money in a pot at the back of the cupboard. So the burglars helped themselves to another £100. (*Show jar.*) Then there was mother's jewellery.

He also helped the burglars by showing them the video and the hi-fi and then, he remembered his dad's shed at the bottom of the garden was never locked. So they helped themselves to his dad's power-drill he got as a Christmas present. (*Show other items and put them in a thief's bag.*)

As if that wasn't enough, this four-year-old helped open the back door while the thieves loaded their haul into the van.

Young Russell then shut the door and went back to his bed and slept for the rest of the night. You can just imagine how his parents felt when they woke up in the morning; certainly a little poorer. And yet, Russell believed these men were his friends. Some friends they were.

That story made me think of a king who thought he would show some people the silver and gold in his storehouse. His name was Hezekiah, king of Judah, and he had been ill. He became friendly with the son of the king of Babylon who sent Hezekiah letters and gifts while he was ill. It's good to send people letters and gifts when they are ill. Do you do that boys, and girls? Yes, Good!

So, the king's son sent messengers to visit King Hezekiah in the palace. I can just imagine Hezekiah saying, "How thoughtful the king's son is to send these nice people to see me. They seem ever so friendly." So they had a free tour of Hezekiah's most treasured possessions in the palace storehouse; his silver and gold, his spices and fine oil and his swords and spears.

Then, later, after the friends had gone, King Hezekiah's minister or prophet popped in to see him. His name was Isaiah. It may be that Isaiah saw these people go into or leave the palace.

"What did those men say, and where did they come from?" asked Isaiah.

"From a distant land," Hezekiah replied. "They came from Babylon."

Then Isaiah asked another important question, "What did they see in your palace?"

"They saw everything. There is nothing among my treasurers that I did not show them." replied Hezekiah.

Can you guess what Isaiah went on to tell Hezekiah? Well, he could have said, "You fool." But he told him that the day would come when Babylon would no longer be a friend of the king's people, the people of Judah. Now that they had seen all these treasures they would be back and they wouldn't have any trouble finding them. And that's exactly what happened, boys and girls. The Babylonians came and took the king's people away to Babylon and also they took all the treasures the king had shown them.

You know, there are people who claim to be our friends and act as if they want to get to know us. But they really want to see what we have and if there is anything worth borrowing or stealing.

Did you know that there are some people who think Jesus is like that? Yes, there are some that think Jesus becomes our friend so He can steal our joy and fun. Some think you can't be happy if you go to church or claim to be a Christian. I can tell you, boys and girls, those who love Jesus are the only ones who have a right to be happy.

Jesus tells us He is the good shepherd who loves and protects us as a good shepherd looks after his sheep. But Jesus also warns us about people who claim to be shepherds but they come to steal and kill and destroy. If they were looking after the sheep, they would steal a few and if a big wolf came they would run away and leave the wolf to eat some sheep.

The devil is like that. He comes along and wants to be our friend but only so he can take away our happiness and take us away from our friend and good Shepherd, Jesus. The devil owns the world's biggest takeaway. Not takeaway food, but takeaway joy.

But we are not going to let him, are we? We are not going to be like little Russell and say to the devil that you can have this, or take that away. Jesus has given us His joy by forgiving all the wrong things we have done. Jesus has given us His peace and His love and it is for us to keep. (Show the three cards and get the children to repeat the words.)

| Joy | Peace | Love |

I wonder what would have happened if little Russell Brown had screamed or ran off to get his parents. The Lord's hand was on his life.

Thieves might get away with things that we own, especially if we are foolish enough to leave the doors and windows unlocked.

But there are others things thieves can't touch or destroy. They are the treasures from the Lord stored in Heaven. All that we have from Jesus today and in the future is safe and secure. Praise the Lord!

Let's have someone read from Matthew 6 v19 – 21.

GUESSING YOUR THOUGHTS
Text. John 2v 25

Materials and Preparation
This talk is ideal for a class of older children who have access to a pen and paper. You can have the instructions written out on a sheet or you can put them up on the board as you proceed.

The aim of this talk is to show the children how Jesus, unlike ourselves, does not have to guess at how we think. He knows what our thoughts really are. I am indebted to Chuck Swindol's Bible Study material on Luke 11 for this opening exercise.

We are going to take part in something you will enjoy and which you can take home to your family and baffle them with the way you can guess their thoughts. If you have your pen and paper ready, please follow my instructions.

1. Pick a number between 1 and 10

2. Multiply that number by 9

3. Now add together the two numbers you got after multiplying by 9. If you only got one number after multiplying by nine, just put down that number.

4. Subtract 5 from that number.

5. Pick a letter of the Alphabet that relates to your number by making
   A = 1, B = 2, etc.

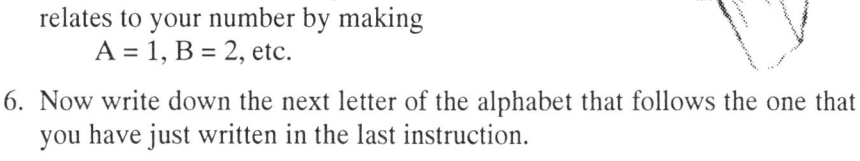

6. Now write down the next letter of the alphabet that follows the one that you have just written in the last instruction.

7. You now have two letters. Write down the name of a country of the world that begins with the first letter and the name of an animal that begins with the second.

There are many countries and animals in the world but I am going to guess your thoughts. My guess is that you have chosen Denmark and Elephant. *(If this exercise has been done properly, instruction No.4 to subtract 5 will always yield the answer 4. The fourth letter of the Alphabet is 'D', which is followed by 'E'. Most, if not all, will answer Denmark and Elephant.*) How many of you got Denmark and Elephant? Yes, I can see I have read the thoughts of most of you. Actually, I have read nobody's thoughts. The simple fact is that the answer is always 'D' and 'E' and most people choose 'Denmark' and 'Elephant'. Try it with the family at home.

It may be that I can't read your thoughts but Jesus claimed He certainly could. It is in John's Gospel chapter 2 we learn that many people saw the miracles Jesus did. I suppose they saw it as a magician's show. They would follow Him to see how many other tricks He could perform.

These people did not take in Jesus. He tells us in John 2 v24 that He would not entrust Himself to these people, for He knew all men and that includes women and children.

Jesus goes on to say in verse 25 that He didn't even need someone to speak for someone else as to their character for He knew what was in a man, or in a person.

Interestingly, John in writing his gospel makes the very next verse, which is John 3 v1 say, 'Now there was a man of the Pharisees named Nicodemus....' If Jesus knew what was in all men, He certainly knew the thoughts of Nicodemus who came to see Jesus by night.

This was no magic trick. This was Jesus, God's Son. This was God living among men knowing their thoughts and actions. And it is the same today. Jesus hasn't changed. He still knows how we think about Him and others. I am glad to say He doesn't condemn us for the thoughts we have that float through our minds. But if we let these thoughts linger there and make us bitter and full of hate, that is wrong and sinful. Also, if we act out our evil thoughts then we again have sinned against God and each other.

We can't help evil thoughts coming into our minds, but we can stop them building a nest and staying there. We can stop them becoming evil acts.

Sadly, today, drink and drugs can cause people to act in a manner outside their control. They imagine they can drive safely when they can't. They imagine they are bigger or greater than they really are. These are people who have allowed these things to disturb their minds and are still held responsible if they do wrong while under the influence of drink or drugs.

Jesus teaches that you become what you think in your heart. That means we all need, like Nicodemus, a change of heart. Jesus thought of it as becoming a new person or being born all over again with a fresh start. That sounds like a really good deal. Let Jesus have a cold heart that hates and through His forgiveness of our sins, He will give us a warm heart that loves.

Perhaps we can't imagine a change in our thoughts about people who have wronged us; or a change in our hearts towards those we have wronged, but it can happen. Not in our own strength but with His help. For some people it happened in a flash when they put their trust in the Lord Jesus; for others it took time for the hurts to heal.

But Jesus knows our thoughts. He knows when we want to make a new start. He knows when we try to put things right and make a mess of it on the first try. His grip is there to help us up to try again. So don't give up when some people don't accept our help or acts of kindness. Many others will see the change in you.

Let's pray about those things that trouble our minds and the change that Jesus can make as one who knows the thoughts we have about Him and others.

Lord Jesus, our thoughts as you well know, are not always kind and good. Things have happened we find it difficult to forget. Lord, you even know the hurts of our lives and you experienced what it means to be misunderstood, rejected, betrayed.

Lord, help us to trust you by renewing our minds, and by giving us a fresh start. Forgive us our sins as we forgive those who have sinned against us. Make us new people by making us more like you.

For Your Name's sake. Amen.

TOTAL COMMITMENT
Text. Romans 12v1 RSV

Materials and Preparation:
Jelly beans are required, enough for all the children at the end of the talk, with one single sweet taken out, while the rest of the Jelly beans are wrapped to look like a good present worth having. Have a board and a knife to cut the sweet.

You will also need one Rolo sweet. Put all the sweets in a bag. Have a card with Romans 12 v1 RSV written on it, or use the overhead for the text.

Hello, boys and girls, I am looking for someone who would like a jellybean today. Do come up. *(Take a sweet from the bag. Have the board and the knife beside you).* Now I would like you to have this jellybean but there is only one problem, I love them too. So I will just cut this in half and give you only a half. Hope you don't mind. Thank you for coming. Please sit down for the moment.

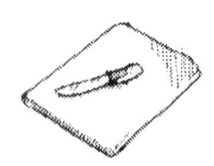

You know boys and girls; I don't know when I last felt this generous. I still have one more sweet to give away. Hands up those who like Rolos. Good! *(Ask someone to come up.)* You really do like Rolos, do you? The problem is, so do I. But anyway, here it is. Oh dear, this is my last Rolo. Now then, that IS a problem. Do I love someone enough to part with my last Rolo? Well, I think I do, or maybe I nearly do. Let me just cut a bit off so I can have a piece for myself. Thank you for coming. Please take what's left and sit down for the moment.

What a generous day I am having. Is there anything wrong with me today, boys and girls? Do you think I was as generous as I could be to the two who came up? What is that, I am not as generous as I could be? Now why would that be? Because I kept something back for myself? Yes, you are right.

Actually, I am more generous than I appear this morning. I just kept something back to tell you what boys and girls can do with Jesus, their Lord.

Some children say, "Jesus, I will give you my life but I must keep part of it to myself. You can have Sunday but I'll have the rest of the week. Lord, I will do anything for you but not when the match is on."

Here is the verse of scripture I would like you to read for me. It is found in **Romans 12v1. I appeal to you therefore brethren, by the mercies of God, to present your bodies as a living sacrifice, holy and acceptable to God, which is your spiritual worship.**

Did you notice the 'present' in that verse? It means 'offer' yourself. But you know the word 'present' can mean something else. Let me dip into my bag once more.

(*Take out the present from the bag.*) Boys and girls, I want to present you with a present, and this time, I don't want anything back, which is just what giving your life to Jesus should be. You don't give a present and then ask for it back, do you? When you offer your body or your life to Jesus, think of it as a present you want to give without wanting to take it back.

Where are the children who were up here and only got part of a sweet? Come up here and help me, please. Would one of you like to open my present? (*After it is opened ask the two children to take a sweet for themselves and give out the jelly beans to all the boys and girls. Say to the two children, "And don't be like me, keeping a part for myself. Give them all."*)

STRAWBERRIES ON A PLATE
Children's Talk on Stewardship
Text. Acts 20 v35

Materials and preparation.
This talk is really teaching children about tithing. You will need a plate with ten strawberries, preferably with the stems still on them and washed so you can eat them. Have them under cover on a table. Also have access to the offering plate or bag. Have a large card or overhead with Acts 20 v35 printed on it for the children to repeat.

This talk is going to be the most difficult one you have ever heard, boys and girls. I think you will understand why when I bring out a plate from under this cover. (*Uncover your plate of strawberries.*)
Now I want to tell you what these strawberries are for.

No. 1 is for my house. I am so glad I had this one because it means I will be able to paint the house a strawberry colour. I will just eat it. Yum!

No.2 is for the car. Just think how well the car will run on strawberries. People will be desperate to smash my car so they can drink the juice. Excuse me while I eat this one as well. I told you this was going to a difficult talk for you all.

No. 3 is for food: strawberry tarts, trifles, jam; you name it and I will have it. Sorry folks, but this one has to go with the rest.

No. 4 is for the family, and as I am part of the family, guess where this one is going? Correct, right into my mouth. You know children this is the best talk I have ever given.

No. 5 is for education. Now I can buy books on strawberries and learn how to make bigger, juicier varieties. "No.5 prepare to meet thy mates".

No. 6 is for sport. I have never really tried kicking strawberries around or catching one, but there is always a first time. I will just throw this one into my yummy net.

No. 7 is for clothes. How would you like to see me in a strawberry suit? I tell you, boys and girls, there will be children coming from far and wide to this place, banging at the door to get in, to see my strawberry suit. I hate to do this but No.7 is about to disappear.

No. 8 is for health. I can't think of a healthier diet than pounds of strawberries and ice cream. Can you? Good! Down it goes.

No.9 is for music. Guess what the music is going to be? Strawberry Fields Forever, by the Beatles. I will just serenade this one down my throat. You know boys and girls, I think I will repeat this address next week.

No. 10 What is this one for? Oh yes, the Lord. The Lord? Not all of it surely. I will just eat the strawberry and give the Lord the stem. (*If you haven't got a stem on the strawberries, just eat most of it, leaving a little piece for the Lord. Put the stem in the offering plate.*)

Well, boys and girls this talk is not about strawberries - it's about giving. It's about how we ought to give to the Lord.

You see children, in the Old Testament part of the Bible we learn about a tithe, which meant a tenth. We learn that the tenth of what people had was for the Lord. The people had to give a tenth of three things: their crops, their fruit and their herd or flocks. The tenth of these things had to go to the priests' assistants, called Levites, who worked in the temple. If anyone couldn't get his animals or crops or fruit to the temple, he offered it in the form of money.

The first person to tithe in the Bible was Abraham. He had to rescue his nephew Lot from kings who were fighting each other. God was good to Uncle Abraham and helped him to get his nephew back and many other things which had been stolen. We are told in the Bible that Abraham gave the Lord a tenth of all he had.

Abraham wasn't forced to do it. He did it because God had been so good to him, and given him so much.

Some people believe that giving a tenth of our money to the Lord is a good way of giving to the Lord today. If you had £1.00 pocket money and you wanted to give one tenth of it to the Lord. How much would you give? Yes. 10p. That means one tenth would go to help support God's work in the church.

Actually, all that we have comes from God, but He lets us use it for all the things I spoke about with my nine strawberries. Can you remember what some of them were for? But isn't it sad, when it comes to giving the Lord something, say one tenth of the strawberries, some people would just give the Lord the stem and keep so much for themselves?

The New Testament doesn't demand us to give a tenth to the Lord, but I always wonder if that is what Jesus meant when He said, "Give to Caesar what is Caesar's, and to God what is God's" (Matthew 22v21). Certainly, the New Testament does teach us to give more when the Lord gives us more, and if we are blessed with money every week, we should give to God's work every week.

The important thing to learn is that you don't give back to God what is left over after you have everything you want. Why is that? Yes, because there would be nothing left. It would be good to get into the habit of putting something aside when you do get your pocket money, and say to yourselves, "Now that is for the Lord." I think a tenth is a good start. Although there may be times when you may want to give all you have to some work for God and for that week keep nothing for yourself.

It may be difficult at first to give, as God wants you to give. Today there are so many children who want to keep so much for themselves, but listen to this; I have never known anyone to give to the Lord's work and not receive a blessing from God.

That may just mean that God helps you feel good or at peace about your giving. That is a blessing. It might mean that God will return to you the money you have given away to help someone who works for God in another country or in the church. It may just mean that you will be happy seeing other people helped by what you have given.

If we love God He will teach us what to do and help us grow up to be generous people who know what Jesus taught, that it is more blessed to give than to receive.

If you had ten strawberries and you wanted to give one to the Lord's work in our offering plate, would you give only a stem? If you had £1 and you wanted to give 10p to the Lord's work would the Lord be pleased if you changed your mind and only put 1p into the offering plate. Of course, He wouldn't. You mustn't let that voice inside your mind tempt you to keep it all for yourself.

Just one more thing you shouldn't do, boys and girls, don't go around telling people what you have given to the Lord or asking others what they have given, to see if you have given more than they have. God knows what you have given and that is enough.

> **It is more blessed to give than to receive**
> Acts 20 v35

Let's finish by repeating these words of Jesus. **"It is more blessed to give than to receive" (Acts 20v35).**

GOD'S FERRY BOAT
Text. 2 SAMUEL 19 v18 KJV.

Materials and Preparation
The text for this talk needs to be from two versions of the Bible, the King James and any modern translation. Have the same texts from each version on a card or overhead.
For effect you could have pictures of different types of boats and ships. You will also need to carry a small child in the congregation. You may want to use the child's father to help you.

I wonder how many of you enjoy playing with boats. How many have a boat to sail in the bath at bath-time? Good! Have any of you been to a boating pond to sail a model yacht? Excellent! How many have sailed on a yacht out in the sea? How many have sailed in a big ferryboat? Yes, quite a number.

Well, today I am going to see if you know what kinds of boats or ships are mentioned in the Bible.

Are there any yachts mentioned? No, but there were small sailing ships which would be as close as we will get to yachts.

Would there be any rowing boats in the Bible? Yes, the disciples trying to row a boat in a howling gale. This boat would be fairly small and could have a sail.

Any big sailing ships mentioned? Yes! There was that one a certain man went on to get away from doing what God told him to do. Do you remember his name? Here is another clue. A great fish swallowed him. Yes! Jonah.

One more question. Any ferryboats mentioned in the Bible? Well, now I don't see as many hands up. Let me tell you something before you decide. There were no cars or lorries in Bible times. Let me ask again. Are there any ferryboats mentioned in the Bible? Many are still not sure.

I see I will have to tell you the answer. It is 'yes'. But it is only in the older Bibles called the King James' Version of the Bible. It is the Bible with the thee's and thou's in it.

Here is the verse. It is found in 2 Samuel 19v18. Now, I'm sure the older people didn't know that was in the Bible.

Let me tell you part of the story of King David; the one who killed the giant Goliath. A long time after that King David had a son called Absalom, whom David loved. I'm sorry to tell you this son tried to take over as king and got an army to fight for him. Which meant David and his men, also his household, had to flee from the city of Jerusalem.

Sadly, his son Absalom was killed in battle and that meant it was safe for David to return to Jerusalem. But they all had to get over the River Jordan. There were women and children to get across. But how?

From 2 Sam. 19 v18 we learn, **'There went over a ferryboat to bring over the King's household.'**

There were no cars or lorries, just people. But ferryboats can carry people as well as cars.

There is a good possibility that the ferry boat mentioned here is the boat that God built, for if you look at our modern translation of the Bible, 'Ferry boat isn't mentioned. It says:

'They crossed at the ford to take the king's household over and to do whatever he wished.' N.I.V.

Do any of you know what a ford is? No, it isn't a car. It is a shallow place in a river where you can wade across. It looks as if the men sent to help David's household to get across did this. (*Lift a small child and carry the child across an area of the platform*) It looks as if the ferryboat was a human ferryboat with men to carry people across. I call that God's ferryboat. He made us to help others who may be in difficulty.

Now, I wonder how you boys and girls could be God's ferryboat. It may be when you are strong men and women you will be able to rescue someone in danger. Some of the older children will be learning lifesaving in your swimming lessons.

I'm thinking though, not of people in water at all. I'm thinking of others who have difficulty at school and need someone to help them over a difficult problem with English or maths or just the difficulty to get to know people. Perhaps God wants you to help them.

Or maybe there is someone you know: a neighbour who is older now and finds it difficult to cross the road. Maybe you older children, who know about road safety, could help that person across.

There may be other children who find it difficult to cross over the door of a church or children's club. I'm not suggesting you lift them up and carry them across, but you could say. "Come with me. I'll come round for you".

I think we can all be God's human ferryboats helping to get others over something they find difficult or unsure about.

Jesus certainly told us that if we help people who are lonely or poor or in other kinds of need it is like doing it for Him. As Christians, let's see how many we can lend a helping hand to this week, as God's ferry boats.

FAITHFUL IN LITTLE THINGS
Text Luke 19 v17

Materials and Preparation
This talk could be told effectively without visual aids but it would certainly be more effective if you found an artist's impression of Moses from children's Bible storybooks.
It would also help to have a card with a drawing of a very long queue of people who would be trying to see Moses. There are many illustrated art books you can buy for church magazines, etc. to photocopy and there are usually crowds drawn for you.
You will also need an overhead or card with a list of little things children can do such as:
> *Clearing the toys away.*
> *Keeping your own toys.*
> *Help to stop fights instead of starting them.*
> *Looking to see if mummy or daddy is tired.*
> *Saying kind things to each other.*
> *Doing what we are told, especially when outside near the busy road.*

Lastly, you will need an overhead or card with the text of scripture from Luke 19v17.

Now, boys and girls, how many of you remember Moses? What can you tell me about him? *(Usually they will tell you about Moses as a baby.)* I want to tell you a story about Moses when he was over 80 years of age. Are there any boys and girls 80 years of age? No? Well, there are some young people of that age in this church.

Think of Moses. He is seated but you can't really see him for the long line of people queuing up to settle fights and things. Of course you children won't fight in your home or school. Or do you?

Well, let me tell you what people might have fought over in Moses' day. Someone would dig a hole, and someone else's animal would fall into it and break a leg. The owner of the animal would say to the one who made the hole, "You had no right making a hole as big as that where my animals are. You give me some money for the animal I can't use."

The one who made the hole might answer, "Your animals are all over the place. They are silly animals and you should teach them not to go near big holes. I won't give you any money." And so it would go on until someone would say, "Let's go and see Moses, he will settle this." I don't think I would like to sort everybody's quarrels. Would you? There were thousands of people with all their different fights, big and small, for Moses to settle.

Moses was getting very weary with all this. Then one day Moses' father-in-law, Jethro, appeared, and just at the right time. When Jethro saw the crowds trying to see Moses, he said, "Moses, you can't handle all these people on your own. There are some big things that go wrong which you could help to put right. Choose other people to sort out the little things" (See Exodus 18v22).

I am glad to be able to tell you, boys and girls, that Moses listened to his father-in-law. Moses looked after big difficulties, while other people looked after little grumps and groans. They looked after the little things.

Could you tell me who looks after the big problems in your home? Yes, Mum and Dad or it could be a mum on her own. Sometimes it is a grandad or grandma.

But here is the good news. You boys and girls can look after the little things. Let me tell you about the things I mean. *(Produce your list as above.)*

When the toys are all over the floor, what could you do to help? That's right, clear them away tidily.

What could you do if you saw someone playing with their toy and you wanted it? Yes, you could ask if you could both play with it and share it. Or you could just play with your own toys.

What do you do if mum and dad are tired? No, you don't waken them up. You try to be as quiet as you can be and let them rest.

If someone is trying to pick a fight, you could try to say something like, "Let's play a game rather than hurt each other".

What do you do when you are out on the pavement and told not to run, but watch the road? Yes, you should listen and obey.

There are many little ways you could help each other and make home a happier place.

Here is what Jesus said to someone who had only a little to look after,

(Show your Luke 19v17 text.) Jesus said, 'Since you are faithful in small matters I will put you in charge of big things'. In this verse in Luke the King gave a man, who looked after little things, ten cities to look after.

That's how Jesus works with us. He watches to see how good we are with the little He gives us to do. When He sees how good we are with the little He puts us in charge of bigger jobs or like Moses more difficult people to keep happy.

Oh, by the way, a little smile would be a good place to start. Let's start today and see how well you are doing the little thing you could look after for your parents or schoolteacher. I even wonder if by next week you could tell me if you managed to do some of the things on my list? I think Jesus would be pleased if you did.

THE FIVE SENSES
A TALK FOR TODDLERS
TEXT LUKE 7 v36 - 50.

Material and Preparation.

As spiritual leader of a Christian playgroup, I spoke to three and four year olds once a month linking into their theme for the month. On this occasion it was the five senses. I was delighted to find that the story in Luke 7 of Jesus anointed by a sinful woman gave me all the senses.

The emphasis is on the five senses but I hope you can see that we can retain important elements of the story for toddlers.

The main link-up with the five senses are:
   Tasting - The Meal
   Seeing - The Woman
   Touching - Jesus' feet
   Smelling - The perfume
   Hearing - Jesus was saying, "You believe in me, you can be good now"

If you want to have objects for this talk, you could have the children with paper plates with a few smarties helping them to enter into the story and taste something.

For the woman you could have a girl acting under your leadership, and a boy acting the part of Jesus.

For the touching, all the children could take their shoes and socks off so their feet could have a touch of perfume. Or you could use the boy acting the part of Jesus.

A bottle of strong perfume would help create the smell filling the room.

My paraphrase of the words of Jesus just needs to be repeated by the children a few times. Then a prayer for Jesus to help the children love Him and be good.

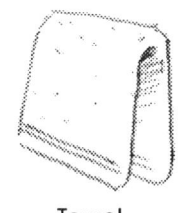

I find it is always a good idea to have them seated as three and four-year-olds on the floor can soon become a rabble.

Lastly, have a little bowl of warm water, a cloth and a towel beside you.

Towel

Bowl of warm water

Well, children, I am so glad to be with you today because I have some things in my bag that you like. I will also need your help to tell this story. You all like a good story, don't you?

Now I wonder how many of you have been to a friend's party. You have? Tell me, did you get a little note or card inviting you to come? Of course you did. Can you imagine what would happen if you heard about a party but you were not invited, but you decided to go anyway? What do you think would happen? Yes, the people would be angry. Yes, there might not be enough food.

Well, this story is about Jesus being invited to a party and like any other party there was food, lovely food. Did you know, boys and girls, that we use our tongues to taste food? So if I tell you that Smarties are yummy yummy, can you taste them? Can you not taste them? Of course you can't! I will just dip into my bag and bring out the plates and I will give you two Smarties each so we can pretend we are at a party and eating the food. Now then, have you got the Smartie in your mouth? What does it taste like? Yes, chocolate and all sugary on the outside. Did you enjoy that? Let me have all the plates back so I can pop them into my bag again. **We taste with our? Yes, tongues.**

Tasting

But let's get back to this story of Jesus invited to a party. Now in those days they didn't have chairs as we do. People would lie down on one elbow with their feet sticking out behind them. (If you were really ambitious you could ask the children to put aside their chairs and use the floor to illustrate your point. But it can be difficult getting control back if the toddlers are unsettled.)

What I want to tell you, children, is that the man who invited Jesus was looking with his ears at someone. Oh no you don't look with your ears, silly me! What do you see with? Yes, your eyes. Yes, it was with his eyes he saw someone come into the party who wasn't invited. Sometimes in those days people could come into a party without being invited. But this woman who came into the house had not been a good lady. She was seen sneaking in just behind Jesus. Oh dear, the man who invited Jesus was not pleased.

But I'm so pleased to be able to tell you that Jesus saw her with His own eyes and He was pleased to see her because I think He had met her before and saw how good she could be. **So what do we see with? Yes, our eyes.**

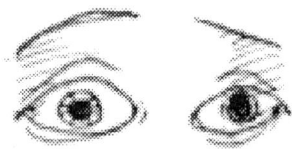

Seeing

You will be pleased to know that isn't the end of the story. Wouldn't you like to know what happened when this lady came in right behind Jesus? Of course you would. Well, she started to cry. She may have been sad about all the times she hadn't loved God or she may have been crying because she was so happy to be loved by Jesus.

The tears began to drop on Jesus' feet. Now in Jesus' day people didn't wear socks. It was just too hot. They wore sandals and took them off when they went into someone's house. So this woman's hot tears splashed on to Jesus bare feet. Splash! Splash! Splash! Jesus didn't mind at all. The next thing that happened... O let's see if there is a girl here with long hair. Can you help me? Good. Is there a boy willing to take his shoes off? I am going to pretend this water I am using to wash this boy's foot is the water from her eyes. My how clean that foot is now. Could the girl with long hair come over beside me, because the woman in my story knelt down and touched Jesus' feet with her hair? Can your hair touch this boy's very clean foot? Yes, it can, but I won't ask you to do what this lady did. She dried Jesus' feet with her hair. I will ask this girl with the long hair to dry this boy's foot with the towel. So she touched Jesus' feet with her tears and her hair. **Is there something else we use to touch people and things? Yes, our hands.**

Touching

So there has been tasting in this story, seeing and touching. Let me dip into my bag again, for this story is also about smell. Who can tell me what we smell with? Yes, of course, our nose. Tell me about this lady in the story. She sneaked in without being invited, right behind Jesus' feet. Anything else? Yes, she wet His feet with her tears and dried them with her hair. Here is a lovely part of the story. She took the very best perfume and emptied the lot right over Jesus feet.

What is this I have in my bag? Yes, perfume. Would you like some on your hand? (Let them all have some to smell.) That was a beautiful thing this woman did. She gave Jesus her love by giving Him the best and most precious thing she had in the house. **So we smell with our? Yes, our nose.**

Smelling

Perfume

In this story there is the tasting of a meal; the seeing of a woman, the touching with the hair; the smelling of the perfume.

33

There is just one more and that is what the woman heard. **What do you hear with? That's right. Your ears.**

Hearing

She heard something very special from Jesus. It was something like this, **"You believe in me, you can be good now."** I think that is what this lady longed to hear from Jesus. The wrong things she had done were all forgiven. Jesus knew she loved him and wanted to be good. Can we say these words together **"You believe in me, you can be good now"**?

And that's how this true story ends. Will you remember that story? Oh, by the way, we taste with our? **Tongue.** We see with our? **Eyes.** We touch with our? **Hands** or hair. We smell with our? **Nose.** We hear with our? **Ears.**

DEN OF ROBBERS OR A HOUSE OF PRAYER
Text: Mark 11 v17

Materials and Preparation
For this talk you will need two sheets of A4 thin white card for each child. As this will become a project for the children to take home or to work on in a class after the children's talk, the cards need to be in an A4 envelope. (You can give this talk without preparing anything for the children to do themselves but to get them involved is more fun and helps them remember the message.) Your first task is to prepare a finished 'House of Prayer'.

On one sheet you need to draw a house. One door in the centre and seven windows would work well for the talk. The windows are cut so that they open out like the windows on an Advent Calendar.

Behind the windows draw various themes for prayer. If you are not confident in drawing even matchstick figures, try and find small pictures from magazines you can stick on the card underneath each window.

In my talk I had a window opening to each of the following:
   1. *The World and missionaries - (A round globe)*
   2. *The Third World - (An empty plate)*
   3. *Friends - (Joined match-stick figures the same size)*
   4. *Family - (Joined match-stick figures but different sizes)*
   5. *The Bible - (Draw a Bible)*
   6. *Thanksgiving (Just the words '**Thank you**')*
   7. *The sick (a bed with someone lying on it.)*

I found it helpful to draw this house on the computer and then enlarge it on the photocopier. Most photocopiers will take thin card but each sheet usually has to be hand fed.

For your talk you will have a finished house with the two cards cellotaped together, the windows cut to open out and the little drawings underneath. Your house will also be coloured using felt-tipped pens.

If you want, you can have another card and draw an eye mask with holes for the eyes depicting robbers, or just draw a bag of money being grabbed by a hand.

I wonder how many of you, boys and girls, have been really angry. What! That many! Would any of you like to tell me what made you so angry?

Did you know that Jesus got really, really angry in church once? The church in Jesus' day was called a temple and it had different areas around it divided off for different purposes. The area where Jesus was angry was called the outer court where people, who were not Jews, could come and pray. These people were called Gentiles. What were they called? That's right. Gentiles.

Now prayer was important to Jesus, so you can imagine how He felt when He found the place of prayer had become like a market where people were buying and selling.

Let me tell you what they were selling in this outer court. They were selling doves. In those days, before Jesus had died on the Cross, worshippers brought animals or doves to the temple as an offering to God. The animal had to be without bumps and bruises. Your animal had to be inspected just as they do at agricultural shows today.

Sadly, there were those who wanted worshippers to buy an animal or dove from the temple even if the one they brought was a good one. So they told people that the animal or dove had something wrong with it. Worshippers could buy doves outside the temple for three and halfpence per pair but to buy the same in the temple cost seventy-five pence. Now three and halfpence was a working man's wage in Jesus' day.

Jesus was angry at these money grabbing animal inspectors who were out to make money out of the worshippers, many of whom would be poor people. He was so angry that He threw these buyers and sellers out of the temple court.

Another thing that made Jesus angry was the high cost of changing the money some people brought with them. The temple tax was a half shekel. So if Jews from abroad came to the Jerusalem temple with Roman or Greek coins they had to exchange them for shekels.

If you had just enough coins to make up to half a shekel that would cost you 1p, but if the coins you gave were worth more than the half shekel and you were expecting change, that cost you 2p. It cost you half a day's wage. Remember a day's wage was three and halfpence.

That made Jesus so angry that He overturned the tables of the money changers and drove them out.

So you can imagine the scene. Here is an area on the outer courtyard of the church meant to be for people to come and pray, where all you heard were buyers and sellers and money changers.

No wonder Jesus said, quoting from the Bible of His day,

"My house will be called a house of prayer for all nations."

Then Jesus continued, **"You have made it a den of robbers."** Mark 11v17.

What does this tell us about Jesus? It tells us two things.

1. Prayer was important to Jesus. He talked about the temple as a house of prayer. I have made such a house with a card. *(Show the children the house of prayer you have made.)*
In fact, this house is a bit like an advent calendar. Do you see how each of the windows opens telling us some of the things we ought to pray for? (Go over each of the drawings or pictures you have in the windows as items for prayer.) Today you can make your own house of prayer to remind you how important prayer was to Jesus and therefore should be to us. And you can take it home and each day open one of the seven windows and pray for what you see in there.

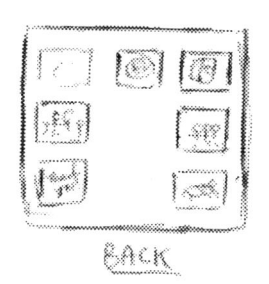

The second thing we learn about Jesus is that

2. People were important to Him. By people I mean, all people, of whatever colour or race. All were precious to Him and all could come to the temple to pray. God's house of prayer was for all nations.

Today let's remember those from different countries who come to our country and don't feel welcome or loved. Pray for those who reach out to them and tell them of the One who loves and welcomes all to His Father's house of prayer. Why not invite someone along to church who feels the need for friendship and a welcome? The church has a welcome for all and is meant to be a house of prayer or a family of praying people. With your 'house of prayer' you can join that family talking to God day by day.

Well, boys and girls, what will it be - **a house of prayer**, (show your house card) or a **den of robbers**? *(Show your spare card with the mask or picture of someone grabbing money.)*

TRINITY SUNDAY

Materials and Preparation

For this talk you will need a picture of a good house. It would be ideal if you had pictures of a house in its stages of building, including plans. Or pictures of an old house and then the same house modernised.

It isn't difficult to put such pictures on an overhead acetate provided you use the thicker acetates that go through the photocopier.

Creator	Builder
Redeemer	Buyer
Indweller	Dweller

You may want to have the words; ***Creator, Redeemer*** *and* ***Indweller*** *on acetate. Also the words:* ***Builder, Buyer*** *and* ***Dweller.***

You may not know, boys and girls, that there is anything special about this Sunday but it is called **Trinity Sunday**. This is the Sunday in the Christian year when we affirm our belief in one God, and also in the belief that God is Three. Three persons, Father, Son and Holy Spirit.

People have tried all kinds of ways to help us understand this belief in one God and three persons, Father Son and Holy Spirit. Many of them have left us still confused about how there is only one God and yet three persons, Father, Son and Holy Spirit all equally God.

The best way I can explain something of what it means, is to let you see some pictures of a beautiful house. *(Show your first picture on the screen.)* Do you like this house? So do I. Now there is a story I once heard a preacher tell, many years ago, about a house just like this. Three men walked past a house like this one.

The first man, as he passed, looked at the house and said, "That's my house." Then walked on.

The second man came along, looked at the house, and said, "That's my house." Then walked on.

The third man stopped at the house and said, (What do you think he said?) Yes, He also said, "That's my house."

Now the three men didn't all live in the house so how could each one say,

"That's my house"? *(Give time for some feedback from the children)*

Let me tell you the answer to this puzzle.

The first man could say, "That's my house," because he was the **builder**. There was a time when the house was nothing like it is in this picture. It may have been a very old run down building or just plans on paper. *(Show any pictures you have of a run down building or even house plans.)*

God, the Father, is like that builder, the creator of the universe. He has the plans for this world and each one of our lives. **In Him we live and move and have our being (Acts 17v28).** And everything He made was good. He is Father God.

Getting back to our story, the second man could say, "That's my house." Because he was the **buyer**. Yes, he bought it. *(Show the finished house again.)* In fact, I can tell you that the buyer, in this story, saw the house getting built by the builder. The builder didn't do anything without the buyer being around. The builder and the buyer were equally involved.

Now that happens today. Someone has a house built they are going to buy and is always around to see what the builder is doing, making sure the builder is doing it right according to the plans.

The second man in the story is a picture of Jesus, God the Son. He was in the beginning with the Father, without Him there wasn't one thing made that was made. Sadly, what God had made got sold out to an enemy the Bible calls Satan. So Jesus had to die on the Cross and shed His blood to buy back people who were created by God but had become Satan's property. When people, young people, older people, ask Jesus into their lives, the devil is evicted, he has to pack his bags and go. He doesn't belong there any more. No longer is that person's life the devil's property.

I sometimes think it would be good, when the devil tempts us to do all these wrong things, to say to him, as Jesus said, 'Get behind me Satan!' or 'You don't belong in my life. Jesus has died for me and bought me with His own blood.'

Let's get back to the story. The first man said, "That's my house." Because? Yes, He was the **builder**.

The second man said, "That's my house." Because? Yes, He was the **buyer**.

But there is the third man who said, "That's my house." He wasn't the **builder** or the **buyer**. He lived there. He was the **dweller**. Now that happens today. A builder builds a house. Somebody buys it, then rents it out for someone to live in it.

But you know, boys and girls, people who buy a house but can't live in it themselves, to begin with, want to have people in the house who will look after it, keep it clean and tidy. Look after the garden. In fact they really want people just like themselves, who love the home as they love it.

So the third man in our story is like the Holy Spirit. He comes to indwell the house of our lives. I also have to tell you that this third man, in our story, knew the buyer and the builder. In fact they were all around when the house was being built.

The third man knew the buyer would be around all the time. But the buyer knew the man who was going to stay in the house loved it as much as he did, and to have him there was like having the buyer there.

And, boys and girls that was what Jesus told us about the Holy Spirit. After He went away He would send another Comforter, someone just like Himself. So, to have the Holy Spirit indwelling your life is like having Jesus with us. That's how we know Jesus and have Him in our hearts. It is the Holy Spirit indwelling us who makes Him known to us and close to us. Jesus said, **'He will bring glory to me by taking from what is mine and making it known to you.' John 16v14.**

Let me see if you have really grasped what I have tried to teach you today. The Bible teaches that God is One. There is only one God. But the Bible also teaches that God is Three, three persons, Father, Son and Holy Spirit.

To understand how these three persons are equally God but different in what they do, I told you the story of the house and the three men. All three can say, "That's my house." The first man because? Yes, He is the **builder**, The second man because? Yes, he is the **buyer**. Then the third man because? He is the dweller.

God the Father created us, but not without the Son and the Holy Spirit being there in the beginning with God. **Remember, through the Son of God, all things were made; without Him nothing was made that has been made. John 1v3.**

Jesus, Son of God, is the buyer of what God has created and of what has been taken over by Satan. He died on the Cross and shed His blood to buy back what belongs to God. The Bible word for that is **Redeemer**. Jesus is our Redeemer.

The Holy Spirit is the **indweller**. Jesus taught, **'You know Him, for He lives with you and will be in you.'** John 14v 17.

To have the Holy Spirit is to have another just like Jesus. Making Jesus known to us. Shedding His love in our hearts. He loves the house of our lives just as much as the buyer.

God is One God. God is in three persons, Father, the **Creator**, The Son, the Redeemer, The Holy Spirit, and the **Indweller**. God in three persons, blessed Trinity.

THE 'n o' 'u o' MOTHERS' DAY

Materials and Preparation
All is not as it seems in the title. This talk is for Mothers Day but we are going to use the letters 'n o' 'U O' (which is n o upside down) to give our talk.

If you are not artistic, have 4 cards, big enough for all to see, with the following words written on them: **no WASHING, no COOKING, no IRONING, no HASSLE.** *Alternatively, have* **n o on** *four cards, big enough, so you can put the pictures of: a washing machine, cooker, iron, and a sad and weary face, inside the* **O** *of your* **no**. *Don't use a capital N for we are really using the shape of a u later on and therefore it is good to keep the letter the same.*

You also need two pieces of card folded in half. Draw the shape of a J on one and the shape of a C on the other in such a way that when you open out the cards the J becomes a U and the C becomes an O. You may want to display your cards on a board or just hold them in you hands.

You are now ready to give your talk.

Can any boy or girl tell me what is special about today? Yes, it is Mothers' Day. It must be wonderful to be a mother. Fathers' Day is never quite the same. I want to help you see what is so special about Mothers' Day. *(Have your folded letters opened out so the letters are n o)* I am now about to reveal what every mother wants for Mother's Day. It all has to do with these two letters which spell? That's right, no.

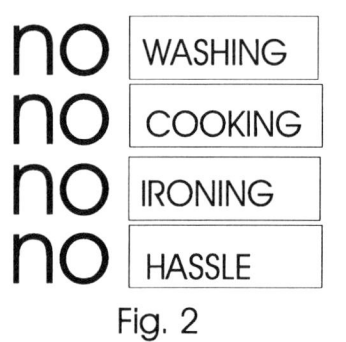

Fig. 1

Mothers are wondering what I'm going to say. One thing I'm not going to say is that there should be no Mothers' Day. Let me show you, boys and girls, what would make Mothers' Day special for many mothers with these letters n o.

(Start displaying your word cards or no cards with pictures inside the O, one at a time)

no WASHING
no COOKING
no IRONING
no HASSLE

Fig. 2

1. Today, they wish there was no **WASHING**.
2. They want to tell you the laundry is closed today. Someone else will have to do it. All children need to keep their clothes clean today.

2. And if there is to be no washing, there will be **no IRONING**. Wouldn't that be special if mum was not stuck behind the ironing board today?

3. Then she would love to have **no COOKING**. Think of the joy of not having to think up even one meal today. Having the meal made for mum and the table set and the dishes all washed afterwards; wouldn't that be special?

4. Well, I don't know if it is possible for mum to have a no washing, no ironing, no cooking, day. What is possible is a no **HASSLE** day. What do I mean by a no hassle day, children. Yes, no fighting, the day going well. No falls. No messy nappies. Well, maybe only one.

Now let me turn the letters **n o** upside down. What do we have now? Yes **u o** and the sound of these letters tells me that Mothers' Day is not just about what happens today. It is about all that Mum has been since last Mothers' Day. It's about what **u o** (you owe) her.

At appropriate point, bend back left of 'u' and right of 'o' to give 'JC'

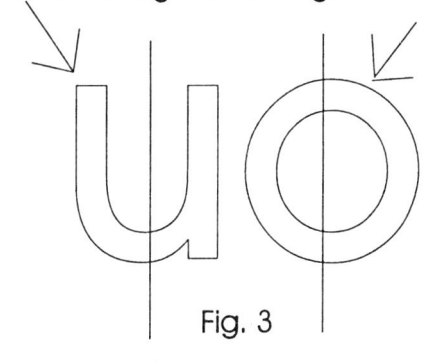

Fig. 3

I would say you owe her **your love**. Don't be like the child who thought it was time his mother paid him for all the things he did around the house and left a piece of paper on the table for mum to see. Washing the car £1: mowing the lawn, £2 Clearing the table, 50p. Tidying my room, £5. He got a surprise when his mum, on the same piece of paper began listing all that she had done, and beside each were the words NO CHARGE. The story ends with boy realising how wrong he had been and going up to mum and giving her a big hug and saying, "I love you mum". I think you owe her your love. The Bible says we are to owe no one anything but love. (Romans 13v8).

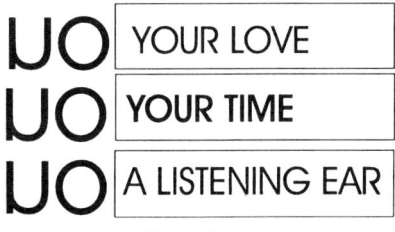

UO YOUR LOVE
UO YOUR TIME
UO A LISTENING EAR

Fig. 4

Then I think you owe her **your time**. Yes, some time to tidy the house, to help in the kitchen. When you give someone your time it is a sign that they are important to you.

I also believe you owe her a **listening ear.** The Bible teaches us to obey our parents in the Lord. When your parents tell you about Jesus and His Love and how He wants you to live, you need to listen. Today you want to listen to what God has been saying through your mum and thank her for praying for you.

I have a feeling that most mums will not get all they desire today. But there is one further point from the letters **U O**. I now want to bend the letter **U** from the left and I now have **J**. Now let me take the **O** and bend it from the right, I now have a **C**. I want **J C** to mean Jesus Christ. As a church of boys and girls who believe, that is our wish for all the mums today. We want to wish you, **Jesus**. You see Jesus cared for His own mother at the Cross. He asked His beloved disciple, John, to take care of her. Mary, the mother of Jesus, was not forgotten by her Son.

Some time later, she was part of a crowd of 120 people who were in prayer, when the Holy Spirit came upon them. That was the beginning of the New Testament church. That's why we wish you **Jesus** on this your special day.

THE TWO SPIDERS
A talk for Missionary Sunday

Materials and Preparation
This talk has been adapted from the story found in the book 'The Story of the Two Spiders' by Raymond H. Belton. Victory Press 1955.
For this talk you need to make two spiders. One nice and fat, the other rather thin and frail. I happened to visit a craft supply shop and found all I required: Two black pom-pom balls, one bigger than the other, eight black 'pipe cleaners' and two pairs of eyes.
It's easy to fix the eyes as they have a sticky back after you peel off the paper. Take four pipe cleaners and twist them at the centre and fix the pom-pom on top of the twist either with glue or sowing them on. Arrange the bends on the legs to resemble a spider's legs. The smaller and thinner spider needs to have the legs bent in unusual ways to give the impression of having had a nervous breakdown. Suspend each spider from a piece of black thread.
You will have to think out how and where to store them until you come to your talk. When you put the two spiders together in the one area they can get entangled, which is the last thing you want.
Finally, you need to make a missionary offering box with a slot on the top wide enough to take your spiders as you slide them in sideways.

The problem with the original story was that it is so short. So I have lengthened it and given it a wider application. It would be advisable to use this talk as part of a whole missionary Sunday programme with a missionary speaking or slides etc.

I am so glad to see so many children on this special Sunday when our thoughts are on those who have left home, family and friends. They have gone to live among people with a totally different way of thinking and living from us. Also a different and difficult language to learn.

How many children here like spiders? Not many. The BBC ran a children's series for very young children about the spider in the bath. Have you ever seen a spider in the bath? Usually you know when someone finds a spider in the house. There is a loud yell or scream. Everyone rushes to the scene expecting to find a member of the family with a broken arm or leg, only to find a spider has been found. Of course it is a gigantic one but, on inspection, it was not the hairy black widow you see in the scary films.

Well, the story I want to tell you today is about two spiders who lived in the church. Yes, these were churchy spiders. They were there, not just on Sundays, but every day and every night.

Now, like most churches, this one had a cleaner, Mrs Clean A Connar. You should have seen her in action. She went around the church like a tank with all guns firing at anything that moved.

She had fly spray with her polish spray. Sometimes she would use both sprays at the same time on some unsuspecting blue bottle or wasp, followed by a severe blow from the Sunday Times newspaper.

I tell, you, boys and girls, Mrs Clean A Connar created such a disturbance in the kingdom of darkness that the insects still alive were all having a nervous breakdown. They were ill.

Now, up in the pulpit area, there lived a spider call Freddy. Let me introduce him to you. *(Bring out the thin spider with the queer legs.)* Here he is, boys and girls. Does he look well? No, he does not. You see Mrs Clean A Connar had been cleaning where the preacher preaches. You know where the Bible sits and the cushion he sits on. Well, poor Freddy had to scamper all over the place to avoid the cleaner. He had nearly lost his life so many times because Mrs Clean A. Connar hated spiders.

It was one such day. The cleaner had just finished and had gone, when a voice was heard. It was Alfred, another spider who lived in the same church. *(Bring the fatter spider out into the open. Hold each spider by the thread.)*

Fred hadn't met Alf before. It was a big church. But Alf was looking so well and fat. He said to Freddy, "My, you look queer. Is it that cleaner?"

"Yes," Freddy replied, tearfully.

Alf, trying to be helpful, said, " You know, I don't think I've ever seen a spider as ill as you are. You need help. You must come and a live with me until you recover."

"Do you mean to say you live in the same church?" asked Fred.

"Of course, come with me."

(Lay the spiders down for a moment.)

Would you like to know where he lived? You would? You may get a surprise. *(Bring out the missionary collection box.)*

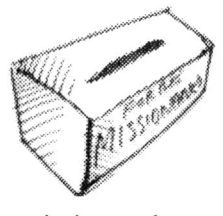

Would you believe it! Alf lived inside the missionary collection box. *(Take hold of the spiders again and place them inside the box.)* Alf said to Fred, "Come in here. Nobody ever disturbs me in here."

That must have meant that nobody put anything in the missionary box.

Today we don't have missionary boxes like the one Alf and Fred went into, but there are ways in which you can give to the work of mission in other parts of the world. Many missionaries rely on their local church for support in prayer and in giving. Sometimes our missionary friends tell us about a special need they have. It may be a scooter or books for the pastors of a church who have very few books.

So from today, why don't we decide to do something that will disturb spiders in the missionary box. Your organisation or Sunday School could, together, have a project for some part of the world. Find out just what is needed and then each child could use an empty Smartie tube and you could fill it with 20p pieces. Just think, if all the children did that we could send the money, or add it to other monies, to help those who have so little.

But the most important thing you can do for our missionaries is pray. What do you think they would want us to pray for?

Yes, pray for their safety, their good health, that people might come to know Jesus. Perhaps two or three of the older children could get together once a month, or more often, to remember in prayer, one part of the world or one missionary or a missionary couple. You can get their prayer letter sent to your home. Then you can tell the church what the needs are, so that others in the church can pray. And, as a bonus, you will have a great knowledge of geography as you learn about the land and the people. For some places there is a need to fill a shoe box with notebooks and pens, soap and toothpaste. In some places, they can't even afford to buy these things.

Another thing you can do, is write. There are many children in other countries who would love a pen pal. Their English might not be too good but you could help them on. And who knows, one day, you may meet up with your pen pal.

One final thing, just remember we can be missionaries in our land, in our area. We can share the Lord Jesus with others at school or at play. Pray and help those who haven't got as much as we have. Here are words from

Jesus that help to disturb Alf and Fred in their cosy box. Jesus said:

The Spirit of the Lord is on me, because He has anointed me to preach good news to the poor. He has sent me to proclaim freedom to the prisoners and recovery of sight to the blind, to release the oppressed, to proclaim the year of the Lord's favour. Luke 4v18 - 19.

He also said:

I tell you the truth, whatever you did for one of the least of these brothers of mine, you did it for me. Matthew 25v40.

It's time to disturb the empty boxes. Watch out spiders, here we come!

WHOLEHEARTED
Text Joshua 14 v 8 and 9

Materials and Preparation
At the beginning, try to get the children to give you the title of this talk by using three pictures. One picture is that of a hole, another of a heart and the final picture is of a boy with ED on his T-shirt.
Then to try and get the message across as to what we are not supposed to be, replace the hole with a half-heart shape.
Have your three pictures placed across a board or pictured on the overhead
Have the words; **WHOLEHEARTED** *and* **HALFHEARTED** *on a card. You may also want to have the words,* **FOLLOW** *and* **CALEB** *on cards.*

I wonder how many children can tell me the theme or title of my talk? Look at the three pictures. What is this picture to the left? It is actually a hole. What is the picture in the centre? Yes, it is a heart. At the right of the heart is a picture of a what? That's right - a boy. Can you tell me his name? It is indeed, ED. So from left to right can you add the pictures together and tell me the title of my talk today? It is **WHOLEHEARTED**. Can you describe for me what a wholehearted person is like?

Yes, Someone who puts his or her whole self into what he or she is doing. A person who gives it all they've got. Or we could say singleminded. Now if I were to replace the hole on the left picture with this (place the half heart shape) what do you think the word would be now? Yes,

HALFHEARTED. How would you describe a halfhearted person? That's right, not all that keen. Not doing a job really well. Not too bothered if it gets done today or tomorrow.

There is someone in the Bible who is known for being wholehearted. He had every reason not to be. Do any of you like spy stories? They tend to be gripping stories, keeping you on the edge of your seat.

Halfhearted

All over the world there are spies who get into enemy country and try to find its secrets; how many weapons it has; what plans it has to invade another country. The spy always wants his or her country to be one step ahead.

Being a spy is very dangerous because you have to disguise who you are and hope that no one finds out you have their secrets before you get back to your own country.

Today there are spy satellites, which can tell a lot about what is happening in a country. Well, this story is about twelve spies. Moses wanted to know if the people in the land the Lord promised them were weak or strong, few or many, and what kind of land they lived in; good or bad. There are many other things he wanted to know. They had also to bring back some of the fruit of the land. So that's why he sent the twelve spies.

They went off for forty days and then returned with the fruit: grapes, pomegranates and some figs. There was no doubt that the land they had spied out was filled with good things to eat. But ten of the twelve spies didn't give a good report about the people of the land. They said, "The people who live there are powerful and the cities are large and well guarded. We can't go in." To the ten spies the men in those cities were big. They were giants. You can just imagine how the people, who heard this report, reacted. There would be murmuring, grumbling and complaining.

But there were two other spies, Joshua and Caleb. Caleb got up and silenced the people. His report was this: "We should go up and take possession of the land for we can certainly do it. The Lord is with us. Do not be afraid of them." Isn't it good to have a Caleb around; someone who moves you on to lean on the Lord and help you do what you think you can't do?

Think of all the people in school, who put you down and tell you, "You can't do that," or "You'll never win in that team." "That's too hard for you." That's when you need to remember the Caleb go-for-it spirit.

FOLLOW

CALEB

I wish I could tell you, boys and girls, that the people listened to Joshua and Caleb's report and went into the land the Lord had promised to give them. The fact is, the Bible says, 'the people's hearts sank'. They listened to the report of the ten rather than the other two.

Well, the Lord was angry with them. He told them they wouldn't enter the Promised Land but Joshua and Caleb certainly would. I like the way Caleb is described in this story. The Lord said of him, **'He has a different spirit and follows me wholeheartedly'** (Numbers 14v24). That's why Caleb would reach the promised land and find what the Lord had promised. He was wholehearted, not halfhearted.

Later on, when Caleb tells his story again, he says, **"... I, however, followed the Lord my God wholeheartedly" (Joshua 14v 8).**

It is my prayer that all of you here will give your lives to the Lord. I hope you will hear His call to follow Him. But there are different ways of following the Lord. You can follow Him at a distance, half-heartedly, or you can follow Him with your whole heart as Caleb did.

All the ten spies could see were the problems, the big cities, the big armies. Caleb and Joshua were of a different spirit. They knew the Lord was with them and that meant they needn't be afraid of the enemy.

Caleb could have said, **'My God is so big, so strong and so mighty, there's nothing that He cannot do.'**

MANY HAPPY RETURNS
Text: Lamentations 3v40

Materials and Preparation

This talk came because I wanted to tell the children about three members of the church who had significant birthdays. If you have a similar situation or a church anniversary, this address would meet that need.

You will need two strips of card of equal length for each child. I simply used a 12" or 30cm ruler, drew around the ruler and multiplied this by the number of children expected x2. Remember you need two strips for each child.

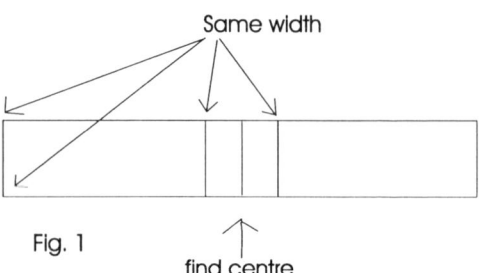

Fig. 1

The thicker the card the better.

You need to find the centre of each arm and then to the left and right of centre draw a line which together equals the width of the strip. (See Fig.1) Tell the children to take the two strips home and join them with glue or staples. Have one already built. In my case the children were going out to their special time after the children's talk and the leader would be stapling them together to make their own boomerang. By taking the end of an arm between the thumb and fingers and throwing to right the boomerang will circle and come back. (See fig. 2)

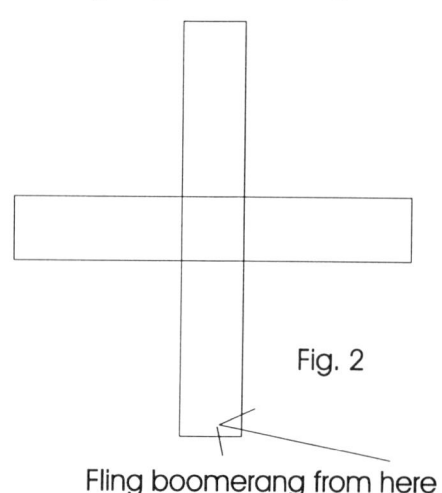

Fig. 2

Fling boomerang from here and throw to the right, slightly angled to the right

You also need a cardboard cut out of the shape of the Australian boomerang (see fig. 3). On the back of it write. "Lamentations 3v40". And have it in your Bible at the verse. This is how I presented the talk but remember it can be used for church birthdays or for the holiday period.

Boys and girls, I need to have you at the front today as I have something special to give you, so please come and join us. Did you know we had three special birthdays in the church last week? I can't give you their ages but I can tell you they are getting younger all the time.

Now tell me what we say to people to have just had a birthday? Yes.

"Happy Birthday". Or we could say something else that begins with "Many..." Yes, "Many happy returns".

What do you think would be the best gift to give to someone to wish them many happy returns? *(Here you have all sorts of suggestions which are usually what the children would like themselves.)* No. These are not the best gifts to wish someone, "Many Happy Returns". Here is the best gift. *(Bring out the cardboard representation of an Australian boomerang from your Bible. Leave your Bible open at Lamentations 3v40.)* A boomerang is the best gift to wish someone, 'Many Happy Returns'. What is so special about a boomerang, boys and girls? Yes, when you throw it, it comes back to you. I can tell you that that is not as easy as you think.

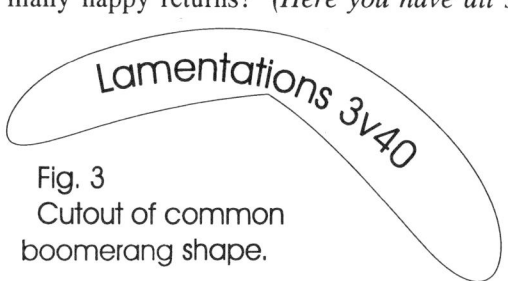

Fig. 3
Cutout of common boomerang shape.

But today, I'm not thinking only of those who have a birthday but also those who need to return to the Lord because they have wandered away from His ways.

You see, children, in the Bible there were those who left following the Lord and did their own thing and went their own way. Sin, or doing, or thinking, or saying wrong things made such people more friends and it seemed it was easier to do what everyone else was doing.

Of course, people found that the way of sin is hard and its pleasures never last. God was not at all happy to see His people drift away from His way. But He had His preachers, like Jeremiah, who would call the people to return to the Lord.

Let me read a verse to you from a book with a long name. It is called "Lamentations" and at chapter 3v40 we read, 'Let us examine our ways and test them, and let us return to the Lord.' I would like you to repeat this verse after me in three parts. Repeat after me, 'Let us examine our ways.' Repeat, 'And test them'. Repeat, 'and return to the Lord'. Is there anyone who can give me the whole verse from memory? Good!

I wonder if there are boys and girls who need to return to the Lord. It may be you used to pray each day. You loved to hear or read the stories of the Bible and you used to like coming to church.

Mr Satan is always there to tempt us away from these things and tell us that it would be easier if we dropped Jesus and church from our lives. He tries to tell us that if we didn't bother going to church, we would have lots more friends.

That may be true, but are they the kind of friends we want to hang around with? Do they help us to be good, or do they lead us into all kinds of trouble? Perhaps it is time to do what our verse tells us, to examine our ways, and test them, and return to the Lord. (You may want to lead them in a prayer at this point.)

Now we can all have 'Many Happy Returns.' The Lord is always there to welcome back those who want to return to Him.

Now as a bonus, you can build your own boomerang today. It won't look the same shape as the Australian one, but, with practice, when you throw it by holding the end of one arm and aiming it to one side with a flick of the wrist, it will circle and come right back to you.

What you need to do is colour it, so that when it flies through the air, you will see a circle of colours. I think you should also have this verse of Lamentations 3v40 written on it.

Oh, by the way, they tell me that if you throw it really hard and it makes Australia, it is bound to come back. MANY HAPPY RETURNS! And a HAPPY RETURN TO THE LORD!

BORROWLAND
A Talk for Palm Sunday

Materials and Preparation
This talk will cause quite a stir in the church. All you need is a bag with books and other items, which you have yet to return to people in the church.

You know, boys and girls, there is an area in Glasgow which is famous. It is called Barrowland, or if you speak Glaswegian, 'The Barras'. It obviously got its name from all the barrows that would be there laden with goods from a needle to an anchor.

Today, they have their own buildings and the goods are in stalls rather than barrows. You can get anything in Barrowland. There is only one problem, you just don't know where it came from. Some say it fell off the back of a lorry or perhaps it was stolen.

I'm not thinking today about Barrowland, I'm thinking of Borrowland because Jesus was right into borrowing in a big way. He borrowed things from birth to His death on the Cross.

1. He didn't have a cot of His own so his foster father, Joseph, had to borrow a manger where the animals found their food.

2. As He moved among people, He was forever dining at another person's table.

3. He couldn't claim any home as His own. In fact, He said, 'The Son of Man has nowhere to lay His head.' Matt. 8v20.

4. When He wanted to preach to crowds on the hillside, He borrowed someone's boat.

5. When He wanted to explain it was right to pay taxes but remain true to God, He didn't have a coin of His own. He had to borrow one.

6. When He died He didn't have a grave of His own. His friends had to borrow a tomb in which to lay Him.

7. He had nothing to leave to His mother but holy memories so He handed her over to John to care for her.

Do you see what I mean when I say Jesus knew all about borrowland? But there is something else Jesus borrowed which I have kept to the end. It has to do with this being the Sunday before Easter. Can you tell me what Sunday this is? Yes, Palm Sunday.

Why is it called Palm Sunday? (Let the children tell you as much of the story as they can.)

So what was borrowed on Palm Sunday? That's right, the donkey. I reckon it is better to borrow one than have one of your own. So many children want their parents to buy them a pony and then later lose all interest in it.

Jesus had a special purpose in riding this donkey. He was showing the people that He was the promised King, who, in the oldest part of our Bibles, was to come riding on an Ass. The verse of Scripture reads like this:

**See your King comes to you,
Gentle, and riding on a donkey,
On a colt the foal of a donkey.'
Zechariah 9v9.**

As you have said, there were people waving palm branches and some branches were laid in the pathway. It looked as if Jesus was being welcomed as a King but, as you know, later people were to cry out "Crucify Him!" "Put Him to death!" They might even have been the same people.

I'm so glad Jesus rode into Jerusalem in such a humble and gentle way. The Lord had need of the donkey and the disciples were to tell the donkey's owner just that if he wondered where they were taking it.

I think if the Lord needs donkeys, He needs you and me even more. He wants others to know that He comes to their lives with gentleness. He comes not to make life miserable but to make it worth living. Even the children sang their praises as Jesus rode past.

Did you know the Lord needs you and me? Did you know you are very important to Him?

Someone once said to a preacher as he started in a new church. 'Without Christ you can't, without you He won't." What was meant was this. Without Christ as King of life we can't do anything that really matters for the Kingdom. But also, the other truth is important, Christ Jesus has decided to include you and me in His great work of showing others His love.

We ought to be so glad the Master or the Lord Jesus has need of us.

> **He has no hands but our hands,**
> **No feet but our feet.**

It would be good to say to Jesus today, "**Thank you Lord, that I am needed just as much as that donkey you borrowed. Use me Lord.**"

I have just one more thing to do children. I have a bag near me. I'm afraid Jesus isn't the only one who has been to borrowland. I have been there too. But Jesus gave back all He borrowed. I haven't. Could a child come and help me give back some of the things I have borrowed from church people and never returned? *(Shout out the names of people to whom the child can give the borrowed items.)*

You know this, boys and girls, I feel better already. But did you know that there are people all over this church who have been to borrowland. What I am going to do is simply this. I am going to ask you to ask your parents to let you help them give back, this week, all the borrowed things they were going to give back a year ago or months ago. And I will have a prize next Sunday for all those who can truthfully tell me that things have been returned. I don't want to know what they all are, although that would be interesting. I just want to know that it actually happened.

(This resulted in a wholesale return of borrowed goods all over the church when I first gave this talk to the children.)

THE 5P EASTER SERVICE

Materials and Preparation.
This is really a programme for a whole Easter service rather than a children's talk. What is explained here needs to be fleshed out for the whole family of the church. You will need a card or acetate with words:

THE 5P EASTER SERVICE
People will obviously think of money but it needs to be explained to the congregation that the main elements of the service all begin with **'P'.** *The children are asked to remember what the parts of the service are that begin with* **'P',** *and you make clear to them that you will give them hints throughout the service.*

You now need five white cards with one of the following on each: **PRAISES, PICTURES, PRAYERS, PROMISES, PRIZES.** *They should be in the order given here with a capital* **'P'** *on the other side of each card, numbered 1 to 5.*
You will also need 6 fluorescent A4 cards

Using only three colours, two of each colour. On these cards will be printed Bible verses which highlight three promises of Jesus and opposite, on similar coloured card, how Jesus kept His promise at Easter.

You also need an A4 fluorescent card to be cut in half along its length with the words **KEEPING A** *and* PROMISE *on the two. Use magnetic tape on the back of the cards. They really stand out against the black metal board. At the appropriate time, down the one side of your board, you will have three promises:*

1. You will rejoice.' **John 16v20.** *Opposite that is:* **"The disciples were overjoyed when they saw the Lord.' John 20v 20.**

2. 'I will come to you'. John 14v 18. (*explain that part of this was fulfilled at Easter*) *Opposite that:* **'Jesus came.' John 20 v 19.**

3. 'Peace I leave with you' John 14v 27. *Opposite that:* **'Peace be with you' John 20 v 19.**

(You may find a problem with the *PICTURE* part of the service as this came from the S.U. Salt material for Easter March 30 week 13 1997. There were two pictures; one entitled **'What Mary expected.'** and **'What Mary found'**.)

In one picture you had Mary sad with the guard at the closed tomb. In the second picture you had Mary glad with Jesus standing before an open tomb. There were also other differences in the two pictures which the whole congregation were invited to spot. These pictures may still be available or you may be able to come up with 'before' and 'after' pictures. If not you can make the service a 4P Easter Service rather than a 5P. Or you may want to use **'PRESENTATION or PLAY'** **describing** *the part the children normally play in these services through readings etc.*

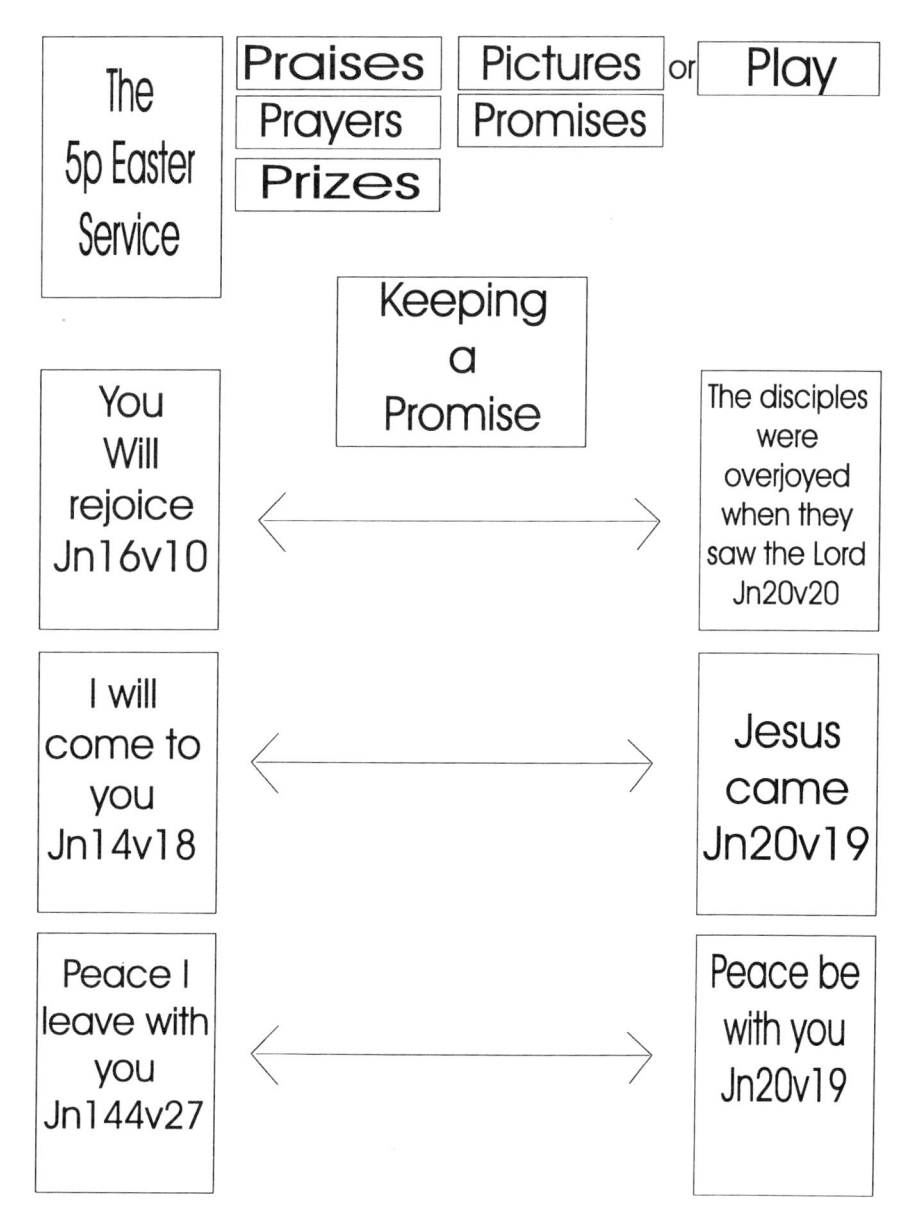

The 5p Easter Service — Praises / Prayers / Prizes / Pictures / Promises or Play

Keeping a Promise

You Will rejoice Jn16v10	⟵⟶	The disciples were overjoyed when they saw the Lord Jn20v20
I will come to you Jn14v18	⟵⟶	Jesus came Jn20v19
Peace I leave with you Jn144v27	⟵⟶	Peace be with you Jn20v19

You are now ready to present the service and the talk. It is presumed that there are other elements in the service not beginning with 'P' such as readings and drama, offering etc. In this book I am only presenting the parts that will relate to the children although it is for the whole family.

Welcome to our Easter Service. I don't think you have been to an Easter Service quite like this. It is called, (*show card*) **THE 5P EASTER SERVICE**. Has anyone ever been to such a service? Good! I'm sure you will all find this one interesting.

I need to explain right at the beginning what a **5P EASTER SERVICE** is all about, just in case you think that is what is expected in the offering. There are parts of the service today which begin the **'P'**. I have cards here. (*Show the five cards with the capital 'P' without letting them see what is written on the other side.*) I want the boys and girls to listen very carefully when we come to these parts because I have Easter eggs for all the children who can remember all five. In fact I am so keen to help you, boys and girls, that I will raise my voice whenever I mention them. Only the children who are sleeping will miss them.

(*Start the service as you want but near the beginning mention loudly the word* **'PRAISES'**.) Did you hear that boys and girls? We are going to sing the **'PRAISES'** of the One who rose from the dead. Let's sing our Easter hymn.

(*At some point after praise you will want to introduce* **'PRAYERS'**.)

Today our prayers are full of thanksgiving because Jesus rose from the grave. (*Prayers according to your tradition.*)

(*After the next song, perhaps, slip in the word* **'PICTURES'**.)

You will see that you have all received a sheet with two Easter pictures. Look carefully, congregation, and tell me all the differences you can see between the two. (*This is not just for the children; parents can help the children spot the differences. Allow a few minutes.*) Well, we do have some very observant folks here today. The important thing is that Mary is so glad to know that Jesus is alive and has spoken her name. She was to rush off and tell the disciples, and Peter, that Jesus was alive. What an exciting task to be the first one to tell such good news.

(*After some other parts in the service, speak out* **'PROMISES'**.) I hope you are getting all these **'P's**, boys and girls. That is the fourth one I have mentioned. Let's put some cards on the board. (*At the top put the two cards* **KEEPING A PROMISE**.) I wonder how many in this congregation have kept every promise they have made. We have all broken promises, I'm sure. But Jesus never did. Not even once. Here are some of his Easter promises from God's word, the Bible. As I put the promises Jesus made down one side of my board, speak them out with me. You will see that these promises were about joy, His presence and His peace. But was Jesus true to His promises? Read out the other verses as I lay them opposite the ones we have here. Yes, the disciples did rejoice. Yes, He did come into their midst. Yes, He did bring them His peace.

(You may want to have other elements before the last part, which brings it all together.)

Well, we come now to our last **'P'**. You will need to guess this one, boys and girls. Here is a clue. I told you at the beginning that if you remember all the parts of the service beginning with **'P'** I would give you an Easter egg. What is another name for giving rewards starting with **'P'**? Yes, **'PRIZES'** Now you have all five **'P'**s, but I don't want you to miss out the others we have had. Let's go over them before I invite you up to find out who has remembered all five. *(Take the five white cards and turn them over and have the children [and adults?] speak them out in the order in which they came but say something briefly about each.)*

'Praises' - Yes it has been good to praise the Risen Lord today as a congregation and as children and young people.

'Prayers' - Did you catch the note of thanksgiving in the prayers, causing our hopes for the present and future to rise?

'Pictures' - My how we did see a difference in Mary when she recognised Jesus, her Lord. To know Jesus makes a difference in every person's life.

'Promises' - How good it is to know that Jesus keeps His promises. And He has promised to be with us to the very end. He will never leave us or forsake us. Trust Him!

Oh dear, what was the last one? O yes, **'Prizes'**. Who would like to come up and give me back all five in this 5p Easter service? *(In a larger group of children you may want to have them just speak them out from where they are seated and give them all something at the end of the service. End the service with another song or rousing Easter hymn).*

MISSING BUT ALIVE
A talk for Pentecost. Acts 2

Materials and Preparation
You will need a child's jigsaw built up but with one piece missing. Have the missing piece to fit in later.

With the computer, or through newspapers, cut out headlines that report something or someone missing. It would be helpful to have missing things and then talk about a missing person.

You will need a balloon that you can blow up and then let go.

Finally, have three cards with the words: A **MISSING PIECE, A MISSING PERSON, and A MISSING POWER.**

Have part of Acts 2 read by older children.

I'm going to take a guess, boys and girls, that you don't know what is special about this Sunday. It is Pentecost. Not as well known as Christmas or Easter but just as important for the Christian Church.

Pentecost was really a Jewish feast coming on the fiftieth day after another important feast called the feast of Passover when the Jews remembered how the Lord had delivered them from the Angel of death by having animals' blood sprinkled on the sides of the door.

Pentecost, fifty days later, was a time of thanksgiving for the grain harvest. A day of great joy. It was that day, when thousands of people were visiting Jerusalem for Pentecost that something special happened. I have some things in my bag to help me tell you what happened on the day of Pentecost for the Christians.

(Bring out the jigsaw with the piece missing. Some of the children's wooden jigsaws can be built inside the box and then tilted up so the children can see what's inside the box.)

What do I have in here? Yes, a jigsaw. How many are into building the really big jigsaws? Good. Well, no matter how big your jigsaw is I think one of the most frustrating times in life is when you have all the pieces connected and then discover one is missing. You have this fantastic jigsaw with beautiful horses only to discover that the missing final piece means one horse has no mouth and another has a stump for a tail.

A missing person

I think you would have an all-out search for the missing piece. Wouldn't you? No-one in the family would be allowed to bring out the Hoover until you had searched under carpets and down the sides of the chair. Then, I can just imagine the beam on your face when the missing piece is found. "Come and see this," I can hear you say, as you point to the completed picture.

Well, what happened at Pentecost was a bit like fitting a missing piece to a picture. *(Place the missing piece in jigsaw.)* You see, Jesus had spent three years teaching His followers how God wanted them to live and what He wanted them to do. Jesus even told them He was going to die and rise from the dead and then He would send someone just like Himself to help them.

Well, around the time of Pentecost, the followers of Jesus were in a room praying; 120 of them by this time. They had built up a better picture of what Jesus meant when He said He would die for them and rise from the dead. These had already happened. But they knew there was a piece missing in the overall picture.

Then it happened. On the very day of the feast of Pentecost, God sent the Holy Spirit. They were gathered in a room with the doors locked because they were afraid. What does this missing piece look like? Well, for these followers of Jesus, it was like a picture of fire and you know how fire shooting up can be like a tongue. It was as if there were lots of these tongues of fire which separated and rested on the heads of all the people. It wasn't real fire; it was a picture they saw. And, alongside that picture of tongues of fire there was something else I will explain in a moment or two. But when this happened the followers of Jesus began to speak in different languages as the Holy Spirit helped them. It was an amazing time.

Those believers began to understand that the Holy Spirit was THE MISSING PIECE *(show card)* in their understanding about what Jesus was telling them God wanted to do in their lives. And, it certainly wasn't to stay behind locked doors.

Let me dip into my bag again. Look at these headlines. *(Show headlines for things that go missing or just make them up).* Do you have things that go missing in your house? So do I. It isn't that anyone has stolen them, I have just forgotten where I put them. Sometimes you have to move house before you discover where something is you lost years before.

But look at this. This headline is not about a missing thing, but a missing **person**. Now that's different from just missing something. Have you ever been in the supermarket, wandered over to the counter, turned around and discovered mum and dad have gone missing? They were there a moment ago. Of course, mum and dad have realised you have gone missing and when they look around the big store and can't find you, are they not glad to hear, through the loud speaker, your name mentioned? "Go to the manager's office" is what they hear. Missing people are more important than missing things. Some people in this country have missing sons or daughters who have gone to another country and have gone missing and every day they hope and pray they will return.

Well, I can tell you the Holy Spirit was not only the missing piece who made the picture complete, He was **THE MISSING PERSON**. *(Show card.)* These followers of Jesus needed The Holy Spirit to be with them. Jesus told them to stay in Jerusalem until the Holy Spirit would come upon them. I don't think the crowd in that room really knew what to expect. But when the Holy Spirit came upon them, I believe they would remember that Jesus said He would send another comforter, someone who would get alongside them and dwell in them.

These followers knew that to have the Holy Spirit dwelling in their lives was like having Jesus with them all the time even although Jesus had gone to Heaven to be with His Father. In fact the Holy Spirit came to make Jesus known to us. He is holy and pure. He is God the Holy Spirit. He is the person who puts God's love into our hearts.

That leaves me with one more thing in my bag I want to show you. What is this? Yes, a balloon. Do you all like playing with balloons? Good. Except when they burst. They can give you a really big fright. The

A missing power

Holy Spirit is **THE MISSING PIECE**; He is THE **MISSING PERSON**, (show cards) but I need to tell you He is **THE MISSING POWER**. Let me show you something. *(Blow up the balloon and then let it go.)* That balloon took off because the air inside started rushing out. What happened after all the air was out of it? Yes, it flopped to the ground, lifeless.

It is the air or gas in a balloon that gives it life and you will all have had balloons that you have to hold on to otherwise they take off and maybe land miles away.

Did you know that when the Holy Spirit came there was more than a picture of tongues of fire? At the same time as people saw these tongues of fire there was a sound. It was the sound of a mighty rushing wind.

Have you heard the sound of a gale blowing through your house or school? It howls. God made sure these believers would never forget the day the Holy Spirit came at Pentecost. There was a power given to these praying people in that room that sent them to unlock the door and to go out to tell the people about Jesus.

Did you know this same power could be ours? We can ask the Holy Spirit to fill us and use us and be to us: **the missing piece, the missing person, and the missing power.**

BIBLE LEFTOVERS
A Talk for Harvest

Materials and Preparation
All we need for this talk are packs of different breakfast cereals. You may need to borrow packs from others. The small variety packs would do but they don't help us underline the main point of the leftovers. It would be helpful to have the following verses on an acetate or card: Ruth 2v14, 18. 2 Kings 4v43, 44. 2Chronicles 31v8, 10 and John 6v12, 13.(Optional) You might want to end this talk with an offering.

This is harvest time, boys and girls. Out in the fields farmers are working long hours gathering in the produce of what has been planted in spring. Fields of hay will have been cut to feed the animals all winter. Also fields of corn which include, oats, maize, wheat and barley. In some farms there will be lots of different vegetables, potatoes, beetroot and lots of other things you love such as carrots and sprouts and cabbages.

Then there are the fruit farmers who bring in the apples and oranges and pears. In Bible times, harvest was a time of rejoicing bringing in the sheaves of corn.

One thing is for sure, without a good harvest we would not have all those wonderful varieties of breakfast cereal.

Now I am going to find out today which breakfast cereal is the greatest and the best loved of all the varieties I have here. *(Go through them one at a time and ask for a show of hands from the whole congregation and try to declare which cereal is the favourite)*

Well, we now know what most people enjoyed for breakfast this morning.

But there is a problem that occurs some mornings at the breakfast table. In fact I would say it is more than a problem, it is a civil war. The fight really starts when one member of the family looks in the packet and judges there is only one helping left.

In our house this would happen with Sugar Puffs. It is the last bowlful in the packet that causes the problem. There are some members of the family who discover the last bowlful doesn't fill the bowl but they rejoice that they got the last bowl of honey coated Sugar Puffs.

But there are others in the family, who shall remain nameless, who look into the packet and measure out a bowlful and discover some left over. Now they reason things out this way. As there is not a full bowlful left for a brother or sister, there is only one thing to do and that is to pile the rest on top of what they have. Which is one of the reasons I like being at breakfast table before the other children. Yes, even fathers have been known to finish the packet. Mothers are supposed to do the same with Special K.

The last thing some people think of are leftovers. Then there are all the grumps around the table. "No, I don't want porridge, mum. It really was Sugar Puffs I wanted. He has enough on that plate for two of us. Greedy thing!" Or words to that effect.

I have come to the conclusion that we are not very good at leaving over something we enjoy for others to enjoy or even the poor to enjoy. And people have been like that for a long long time.

Let me tell you of three groups of people who could thank God for leftovers.

1. First there are Ruth and her mother-in-law Naomi. *(Read part of the two verses)*

> Ruth and Naomi

...When she sat down with the harvesters, he (Boaz) offered her some roasted grain. She ate all she wanted and had some left over. Ruth 2v 14.

...Ruth also brought out and gave her (Naomi) what she had left over after she had eaten enough. Ruth 2v 18.

Twice Ruth could thank God for leftovers. Her mother-in-law's friend, Boaz, left Ruth some sheaves of corn the reapers left for the poor people. She would gather the sheaves into the large skirt of her robe.

She could also thank God for the leftovers of roasted grain. She had eaten enough so she took what was left over for Naomi.

You see, God had written it into His law that the farmers should not forget the poor people, those who didn't own land. They were not allowed to cut the corners of the field but leave some for the poor.

2. The second group of people was Elisha and his servant. *(Read 2 Kings 4v42- 44)*

> Elisha and his servant

A man came from Baal Shalishah bringing the man of God (Elisha) twenty loaves of barley bread baked from the first ripe corn, along with some ears of new corn.

"Give it to the people to eat," Elisha said.

"How can I set this before a hundred men?" his servant asked.

But Elisha answered, "Give it to the people to eat. For this is what the Lord says: They will eat and will have some left over."

Then he set it before them, and they ate and had some left to over, according to the word of the Lord *(2 Kings v 42-44)*.

I wonder how many know there was a smaller miracle in the Old Testament of feeding a hundred hungry men with 20 barley loaves. Here we have a hundred hungry men fed and yet Elisha's servant saw some bread left over. I think the Lord wanted them to have their share of the bread for helping God work a miracle. They gave it out and God made it last. God can do that, you know. Can you remember how He did it in the New Testament, about a boy with loaves and fish? Yes, Jesus prayed. The meal multiplied and over 5,000 were fed. And there were how many baskets of bread left over? Yes, twelve. **See John 6v12-13.** *(In the feeding of the 4000 there were seven baskets left over.)*

3. Here is the last group of people who could thank God for the leftovers. We have had Ruth and Naomi, Elisha and his servant. This time it is a King and his officials. King Hezekiah.

> Hezekiah and his officials

King Hezekiah wanted people to worship the true God again. People had started to worship gods of stone and metal. He got the people to smash these down and to bring their gifts to the temple to thank the Lord and worship Him as the true God again. But the people brought so much it just heaped up an up.

When Hezekiah and his officials saw the heaps they praised the Lord and blessed His people Israel. (2 Chron. 31v8.)

And Azariah the chief priest, from the family of Zadock, answered, "Since the people began to bring their contributions to the temple of

the Lord, we have had enough to eat and plenty to spare, because the Lord has blessed His people, and this great amount is left over" (2 Chron. 31v10).

This is a remarkable story of the people of God so moved to give to the Lord that they found they were none the poorer for giving a tenth of everything to the Lord.

I wonder what would happen if boys and girls and church members and friends all gave a tenth of what they had to the Lord? The Bible teaches that such people would not be without food and all they need, and there would be the leftovers to bless so many others.

Three groups of people who could thank God for the leftovers. Do you remember who they were?
        1. Ruth and Naomi
        2. Elisha and his servant
        3. Hezekiah and his officials.

(A good way to end this address would be to direct some kind of giving to the poor in a given country. Or explain where the harvest fruit etc. will go.)

HOW LONG WILL IT LAST?
(A talk for All Saints Day)
Text Matt. 25v21 'Well done, good and faithful servant...'

Materials and Preparation

For this talk we need a few things that last for a certain length of time. You may want to bring a big sweet or gobstopper and ask the children how long they can make it last. Or bring out chewing gum and ask how long they can make that last. You may want to talk about the goldfish and ask how long has it lasted when you forgot to feed it. You are trying to make the point that some things don't last very long while others things stay with you or the family for a long time.

For this 'All Saints Day' read up on the story of Polycarp of Smyrna who was martyred for his faith in AD156. The words of Polycarp we want to emphasise are these: 'Eighty and six years have I served him, and he has done me no wrong; how then can I blaspheme my king who saved me?' Have these words on a card or on the OHP. You need a separate card with the name **POLYCARP** on it. You may want to put **BISHOP POLYCARP.**

A good way of starting an All Saints Day address for children is to get them to guess the special Sundays of the Christian Year giving a sweet to those who get the different Sundays in the year. They don't often come up with 'All Saints Day' which means you can explain the true meaning of Hallowe'en as All Hallows Eve or All Saints Eve.

You have done well, boys and girls, telling me how long you make things last and telling me about those special Sundays in the year and about this Sunday as 'All Saints Day'.

Today I want to tell you a story about an older man who made something last a long long time. He was a saint, and a saint in the Bible is anyone who loves the Lord Jesus and will live and die for him. Let me tell you this man's name. He was called Polycarp. *(Hold up the card).* That is an unusual name.

He was one of those who, as a child, knew John the disciple of Jesus. I can just imagine him sitting at old John's feet, for John would be very old by this time. He would listen to John tell the stories of Jesus and teach him how to be a faithful follower of the Lord Jesus. Ploycarp had a pal and the two of them used to listen to John tell his marvellous stories.

Well, time went on, and Polycarp felt he wanted to lead a church. Later the church made him a bishop and he had to look after the church of Smyrna in Asia.

Now you might think that being a bishop is a wonderful job; looking after churches and working only one day a week. I have to tell you that bishops and ministers work more than one day a week. And I have to tell you that when Polycarp was bishop Christians were being asked to buy idols and worship Caesar the Emperor and call him Lord.

Polycarp told the Christians not to buy idols or worship Caesar as Lord. Jesus was their Lord and no one else.

Well, you can imagine how angry the people were when the trade in idols was not going well and when these Christians would not accept Caesar as their Lord.

The people of the city started to shout for Polycarp to be arrested and killed for encouraging Christians to disobey the state.

The mounted police managed to find out where Polycarp would be. It was late in the evening when they came to arrest him. When Polycarp heard them at the door, he came down from his bed and ordered that the police be given something to eat and drink. Such was the kindness of the man, who by this time was 86 years of age.

Polycarp asked that he be allowed to pray for an hour before they took him. They agreed. In fact, he prayed for two hours. The police where so impressed by this man's love for God and others that they felt sorry about having to come and arrest him.

They put him on an ass and led him into the city. The authorities tried to make Polycarp say "Lord Caesar" but he wouldn't. They put him in the arena where they could let loose a wild beast on him, but still Polycarp wouldn't worship anyone except the Lord Jesus. They threatened to burn him alive, but still he wouldn't deny His Lord. In fact, here is what Polycarp said that we should remember:

"Eighty and six years have I served him, and he has done me no wrong; how then can I blaspheme my king who saved me?'

You see, children, Polycarp made something last a long, long time and that was his faith in the Lord Jesus. From a boy right up to his eighty-sixth year. All those years he found the Lord to be so faithful to him and he would not let His Lord down even if it meant dying for His Lord. They took Polycarp and he was killed for Jesus. He was a faithful servant all these years.

We asked at the beginning how long we can make something last. I wonder how long your faith in Jesus will last. Some people here can remember how they began to trust Jesus as their Lord and Saviour when they were just children in the Sunday School and perhaps someone in their family said, "It will never last". And they can tell you today that it does last. In fact, unlike sweets and chewing gum, Christians have the Lord to help them continue in the faith. He is the One who is able to keep us from falling.

I think Polycarp would hear from heaven those words of Matt. 25v 21 'Well done, good and faithful servant. Come and shared your Master's happiness.' On this special Sunday let's remember those Christians today, those saints, who suffer for their faith or have been killed and let's ask the Lord to keep us faithful to the end.

(Open Doors ministries have a lot of information about the suffering Christians and those who have been killed for their faith. Some of the older children could write out a prayer for one or two of them.)

THE ELEPHANT NEVER FORGETS
Luke 2v41-52
A Talk for Remembrance Sunday

Materials and Preparation

You will need either a copy of the Walt Disney Jungle Book video or the Jungle Book story book by Rudyard Kipling.

What would be ideal is to show a clip from the video where the elephants are about to march with the colonel leaving his son behind up to the point where he turns to go back for the baby elephant but forgets to shout, "Halt".

If you can't do that then just show the front cover of the video or the pictures in the book. Have two cards with the words **HIS SON** *and* **HALT**.

What is your favourite Walt Disney video, boys and girls? My favourite is Jungle Book. Whenever it is on for children in the house I find I must stop and watch it myself. And you know what? I have watched it lots of times and I can tell you what scene follows each scene. But I still watch it.

Tell me, what is your favourite character in the story? I like the bear with his song 'The Bear Necessities'. Anybody like the vultures with their song 'We are your friends'? Good.

The characters I want you to think about are colonel, the elephant, and the dawn patrol. They seem to waken everybody up when they are on the march. The ground shakes beneath their feet. (At this point show the clip or continue as follows.)

Do you remember that part where the elephants are about to march off and Winifred, the colonel's wife says to him, "Haven't we forgotten something?" Do you remember how the colonel replied? "Nonsense, old girl, an elephant never forgets."

Well, that may be true when they teach elephants trick in the circus but in this story, what had the colonel forgotten? Yes, **HIS SON** *(show card)*. He was going to march off without his son. That wasn't very thoughtful, was it?

His son

Do you know that happened to Jesus once? He was twelve years of age when Mary and Joseph took him to Jerusalem for the special feast called The Passover. There would be many others travelling with them the sixty miles from Nazareth to Jerusalem. After a week in Jerusalem it was time to go home but Mary and Joseph didn't notice that the boy Jesus wasn't with them. When they did wonder where he was, they weren't worried. They thought he must be in the crowd travelling with one of his young friends.

But He wasn't in the crowd with His friends. They had set out three days without him. They just had to about turn and go back to Jerusalem and find Him.

Do you remember where they found Jesus? Yes, in the temple sitting with the teachers listening to them and asking them questions.

His mother said to him, **"Son, why have you treated us like this? Your father and I have been anxiously searching for you."**

Do you remember how Jesus replied? **"Why were you searching for me? Didn't you know I had to be in my Father's house?"**

The Bible then tells us that Mary and Joseph did not understand what he was saying to them. But Mary, his mother, treasured all these things in her heart.

Mary and Joseph aren't the only ones who forget about Jesus. Many people today don't think about Him. It took Mary and Joseph three days to find Him but we can find Him today and by prayer invite Him to be our friend and travel guide through life. He is no longer a boy but a man who went to the Cross to die for you and me to take away our sin and He rose from the dead, and went to be with the Father He spoke about as a boy. But today, when we ask Jesus into our lives, He makes His presence known to us. Boys and girls, find Him today.

Getting back to the story in Jungle book. What had the Colonel elephant forgotten?

Yes, his son. But there was something else he forgot. He had his soldier elephants right about turn to go back for his son. When he found him the colonel had forgotten something else. Do you remember what it was? He forgot to say **HALT!** (*Show card.*) 'Do you remember how all the elephants piled up on each other? I think the colonel was having a bad

| Halt |

day remembering things. He forgot his son and he forgot to say halt.

Can anyone tell me what is special about this Sunday? Yes, it's Remembrance Sunday and there are two things I want you to remember on this special Sunday taken from the Jungle Book story.

Don't forget the sons and daughters who have given their lives in world wars and other wars since 1945. On this Sunday we talk about the sons of a community or a town who were killed in battle. In every town there is a stone monument with their names engraved for all to see. We call that stone monument the Cenotaph. That means their names are there but they are buried at some other place.

So, unlike the elephant, we mustn't forget the son of a family or the sons and daughters of a community who gave their lives for our freedom.

But also, unlike the elephant, we must remember to say 'Halt!' I don't mean 'Halt!' as if we are on a march, but we need to say 'Halt!' to those who always want to fight. Families and school pupils have to learn that God made us for peace not war.

Nations of the world have to learn that destructive weapons can't blast us into loving each other. There is always a better way, the way of love and peace.

I'm so glad Jesus is called the Prince of Peace.

You know, boys and girls, in some countries there have been thousands who have said we have had enough trouble and fighting and killing. They have taken to the streets with no weapons, thousands of them. The soldiers have been ordered to fire on them but they wouldn't. Instead, those who were causing all the trouble, were taken from their position of power and that power given to others who love peace. The people by their marching had risked their lives for peace. By their action they said, 'Stop this violence. Halt this killing. We want peace.'

What two things did the elephant forget?

Yes, **HIS SON** and to say '**HALT!**'

What two things must we remember this Sunday? Yes, the sons and daughters who were killed during the past wars.

And to say, 'Halt!' to those who always want to fight and kill. And to know Jesus, the Prince of Peace. Love always finds a better way.

A WORD IN SEASON
A talk For Advent
Text Galatians 4v4 John 14v 2-3

Materials and Preparation

For this talk you are going to make use of the word **ADVENT** *so each letter needs to be drawn on card. Fluorescent card would be ideal. There are a few different ways you could present this talk. You could use a black metal board with magnetic tape behind each letter, or you could have a piece of solid wood with a deep groove along its length which needs to contain all the letters of the word and wide enough to allow you to slip letters in and out of the groove. If you go for the second option the card needs to be as thick as you can cut. Using the magnetic board the card can be thin.*

You may want to have children read the few verses at the end, and you may want to have the Latin words on a card.

I would present the talk with the letters jumbled up and get the children guess what the word might be.

Well, boys and girls, we have come to the fourth Sunday before Christmas. Can any of you see a word in the jumbled letters, which tells us what we call the season before Christmas?

Here is a clue. You get calendars for this season with little windows you can open up each day. Yes. It is the season of **ADVENT** *(sort out the letters to spell the name)*. What I want to try and do today is tell you something about what **ADVENT** means.

The first thing I am going to do is take away the **'V'** and then I want to put the **'T'** where the **'D'** is, and put the **'D'** where the **'T'** was. Now can you tell me what two words I have now? Yes, **AT END**

That's the first lesson we need to learn about **ADVENT**. It has to do with the end of something, namely the Christian Year. All during the year churches have been thinking about Jesus' life and work. They have thought about Christmas, then the baby Jesus being brought to the temple, His baptism and temptation in the wilderness, His miracles and parables.

All churches think of a special week in Jesus' life called **Passion Week**, which starts a week before Easter Sunday with Palm Sunday. During that week we have Good Friday and then on to Easter Sunday and the resurrection of Jesus from the dead. We also think of Jesus sending out

Jumbled letters of │A│D│V│E│N│T│

Then reassemble in the order below:

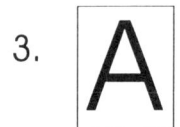

1. │A│D│V│E│N│T│

2. │A│T│   │E│N│D│

3. │A│

4. │A│D│

5. │D│V│

His disciples into the world and also His ascending into Heaven. So at **ADVENT** we are **AT** the **END** of another Christian Year with all its events in the life of Jesus.

This time I am going to take the letter 'A' on its own because this letter reminds us of a beginning. What is the letter 'A' the beginning of? Yes, the alphabet. But for today I want it to remind you that although Advent may mark the end of the Christian Year it also marks the beginning of a new **Christian Year.**

We start the Christian Year reminding ourselves that hundreds of years before Jesus was born, people called prophets foretold that someone called 'The Messiah' would come, whom God would raise up to save His people.

Before Jesus came, for around four hundred years, there were no prophets reminding the people about God's promise to send His special agent called the Messiah. But God was true to His word. Jesus came. Another prophet starting preaching about the Messiah. His name was John the Baptist. He was the one who pointed people to Jesus.

So, **ADVENT** is about an ending and a beginning. The end of one Christian Year of remembering the life and death of Jesus, and the beginning of a new Christian Year.

This time I want to put another letter beside the **'A'**. I am going to place a **'D'** alongside it. Have any of you seen the letters **'AD'** together? Good. Some of you will have seen these letters in a newspaper where people are trying to sell things. But what I am thinking of is an abbreviation for two Latin words. **'Anno Domini'** Can any clever person tell me what that means? It means **'In the year of our Lord'**.

ADVENT, pointing as it does to the coming of Jesus into the world, is going to introduce us to a Jesus who would change our system of dating. It took around six hundred years before a monk called Dionysius Exiguus started dating history using **AD**. For this monk Jesus' coming to this earth marked a new way of thinking about the importance of Jesus. From now on history is either **BC**, which means? Yes, **Before Christ** or **AD**, which has come to mean, **'After Christ'**.

Let me move the **'A'** away from the **'D'** and put another letter after the **'D'**. This time I will use the **'V'**. Most of you will not know that some older Christians, when they are writing a letter and add that they hope to see the person soon, put **DV** after what they have said. Have you any idea what they mean by **DV**? What they mean is 'God willing'.

DV is from another two Latin words, **DEO VALENTE** which means, 'God be willing', or 'by God's will'.

You know, boys and girls, **ADVENT** is also about God's will, God being willing to come as a human being in the person of Jesus. God knew that we couldn't reach up to the goodness He wanted to see in us. He saw how much we struggled to be good on our own and how much we failed in the attempt. Someone had to come and save us from all the wrong things we did. But it is important to learn that when Jesus came as a babe, that was really God with us. Jesus was God the Son; a God who was willing to come and become one of us. He was willing to come but also willing to save all that come to Him through the Lord Jesus. **DV** says, God be willing'; **ADVENT** says 'God is willing'.

Well, I have come to the close of my talk. I have done something, with all the letters in the word **ADVENT** to help us understand what this season means.

Let me go over what we said. We started with:

ADVENT

We dropped the **'V'** and exchanged the **'D'** and **'T'**. What did that give us? Yes,

AT END

Can you tell me what was at an end?

Yes, the Christian Year of events in the life of Jesus.

We then used the letter, **'A' which** is the beginning of the what? Yes, the Alphabet. But also to remind us that **ADVENT** is the beginning of? Yes, a new Christian Year of thinking more about Jesus.

Next we added **'D'** to the **'A'** and got **'AD**.

Which reminded us to put an AD in the newspaper? No, it told us that a holy man, 600 years after Jesus, thought Jesus was so important that we should date our history, 'In the year of our Lord'. You see, all history is **HIS STORY.**

We then took away the **'A'** and put a **'V'** after the **'D'** to get **'DV'** which means? Yes, 'God be willing'. In **ADVENT** we learn that God was willing to come as a man in the person of Jesus. To suffer and die so that we might be saved from our sin.

<u>And, boys and girls, if Jesus came as promised at the right time</u>

**But when the time had fully come,
God sent His Son. Born of a woman, born under the law.** Galatians 4v4

then believe me, He will come again as he has promised.

**In my Father's house are many rooms,
If it were not so, I would have told you. I am going there to prepare a place for you. And if I go and prepare a place for you. I will come back and take you to be with me that you also may be where I am.**
John 14v 2,3

CHRISTMAS CRACKER
Christmas Day Talk

Materials and Preparation

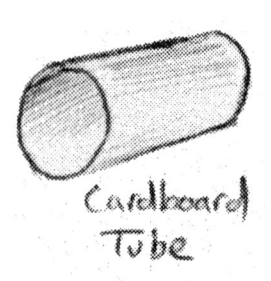

You will need to make a cardboard tube big enough to contain the following items:

A small doll, a Christmas Praise Tape, a paper banger, a joke book or page of jokes, a crown-shaped paper hat, and chocolate as a prize with the hat. The tube size will vary as to whether you have a book or a sheet of paper and according to the size of the banger. It doesn't really matter if it is fairly big. Secure the ends of the tube so that when two children pull it the contents don't all fall on the floor. Wrap the whole thing in crepe paper, twisting the ends like a cracker, and have some questions relating to the Christmas story so you can give away the items that you have brought.

With the exception of the tape and the Joke book nothing should be too costly. I gave away a tape of carols I didn't want. There are books of funny stories in Christian bookshops, which don't cost the earth. The doll was a small cheap one.

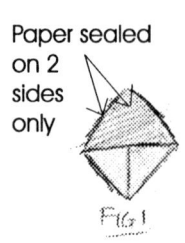

To make the banger. Cut a piece of card into a square. Paste Christmas paper over one side of the card. Place it before you as a diamond shape. Bend it in half so that the folded card is now triangular in shape. Open it again and glue some strong brown paper over half of the diamond shape. Fold it again and hold the end, which has no brown paper, give it a strong flick downwards, and it should bang. Place it inside the cracker.

The idea is to have what you would normally find in a Christmas cracker. The only exception is a praise tape. Most crackers have a toy, a joke and a hat. But each item in this cracker speaks of the real Christmas story.

Have the cracker hidden somewhere.

It is Christmas Day and I can see you have had a wonderful Christmas with all the toys in the church today.

Today I have brought something with me. Would you like to see it? I will just bring it out of its hiding place. What do you think of this cracker? Is it not a cracker of crackers? I don't think you will see one this big at the dinner table today.

So, what is the first thing you do with a cracker? Yes, you pull it. Can I have two strong children to pull this cracker? (*It can take a bit of pulling. The tube will hit the floor. Lift it and place it on its end on a table.*) You would notice, boys and girls, that there was no bang but I have a surprise for you at the end of this talk.

Now tell me some of the things you get in a Christmas cracker? Good. Well, most of the things you get in a cracker are in this big one but each one reminds us of what we have been hearing over the last week or so.

Let me open up the end of the tube. (*Bring out the baby doll*) This is the toy in my cracker. It's a baby doll.) Now we all know that the Christmas story is about the baby Jesus coming into this world as our Saviour and Friend. We must always keep Christ in Christmas because without Him there would be no Christmas. I hope that message got through to all of you this year.

I feel so generous that I would like to give this little doll to some girl today. But there is a question you must answer and your parents can help you with the answer.

When Mary was expecting her baby, she went to see someone to tell her the news. The lady she went to see was also expecting a baby and when she heard the news the baby within her leapt for joy. Who was that lady? Yes, Elizabeth.

Let me dip into the tube for something else. Oh yes, it is a paper hat. I will open it out. What kind of hat is it? It is a crown. Who would normally wear a crown? Yes, a King. You know boys and girls, another message we have been trying to get through to you all is that Jesus came as a King. He was King of the Jews. That was part of the title over the Cross, on which He died; **Jesus of Nazareth, King of the Jews.**

But Jesus wasn't like other kings. He didn't come to gather a mighty army with weapons to kill. He came to bring in a New Kingdom of people who would do what is right and a kingdom of joy and peace. Don't forget boys and girls, that Jesus wants to be King in our lives. We need to be able to say to Him, **"Jesus, reign in me".**

Now I am going to ask the boys a question this time. If you get it right you can have this well-sought-after hat. Oh, by the way, there is a bar of chocolate going with the hat.

When the Wise Men came to Jerusalem, they asked a question which disturbed King Herod. What was that question? Yes, **Where is He who is born King of the Jews? Matt.2v2.**

It's time to dip into my tube again. *(Bring out the praise tape)* Now this is something we don't normally get in a cracker. But the Christmas story would not be complete without it. It is a Christmas Praise Tape.

Another message we have been trying to teach you is that the shepherds heard heavenly praise. The shepherds returned after seeing the baby **'glorifying and praising God for all the things they had heard and seen'. Luke 2v20.** Then we mustn't forget that Mary rejoiced when she heard she was to bear this precious child.

She quoted from a song she knew, **"My soul glorifies the Lord and my spirit rejoices in God my Saviour". Luke 1v46, 47.**

Then as we have said, Elizabeth's baby leapt for joy when Mary told her the good news.

We mustn't let anything in our modern Christmas rob us of our praise to God for sending Jesus. It is there in the beginning and it needs to be there today.

I want to give this tape of Christmas praise to some home or family, so here is the question.

In the story of the Wise Men, who was anything but joyful when he heard about the birth of the baby King? Yes, King Herod.

I must dip into the tube again. Oh yes, you will like this. No cracker is complete without a joke or funny saying. I have a book full of funny stories for some home. Here are some from the book. *(Tell a few funny stories from the book. The following books offer good stories:*

Three books by Rev. James A. Simpson Published by Gordon Wright. 25 Mayfield Rd. EH9 2NQ Edinburgh. **Holy Wit, More Holy Wit and Laughter lines.**

Two books by Stephen Gaukrodger and Nick Mercer, Published by S.U. ***Frogs in Cream** and **Frogs 2.***

*There is also **Joe's Jokes**, and **More Joe's Jokes**, a minister's mirth published by Burning Bush Publications 134, Ballynahinch Rd. Lisburn, Co. Antrim BT 27 5HB.*

I am going to give this book away if someone can answer the following question.

It isn't true in the carol that shepherds washed their socks by night. What should it be? Yes, **While shepherds watched their flocks by night.**

Well, that's it. Or is it? What did you miss at the beginning when you pulled the cracker? That's right, the bang. I said I would have a little surprise at the end. We can end with a bang, if we can't begin with one. Are you ready for this? (*Take the folded card and quickly flick your arm and wrist for the bang*).

Now I know there are many parents who would dearly love to have one of these in their home today. Maybe not! Well, there must be many children who would love to have one of these. One final question.

This Jesus who came at Christmas, lived as our example, died for our sins on the Cross, rose from the dead, is now in Heaven with the Father praying for us. Is that the end of the story of Jesus coming to this earth? That's right. It isn't the end. The Bible teaches us He is coming again. He came the first time. Be sure He will come again.

THE END - SAD OR GLAD
FOR LAST SUNDAY OF YEAR

Materials and Preparation.

This talk is for the last Sunday of the year. You will need five objects plus a series of cards with Bible verses on them. The first object can be just a white rectangular card on a board representing a cinema screen. For this part of the talk you will need a felt tip pen. The second object is the end of a chocolate biscuit, or the last bite, wrapped in its proper wrapper. A book is required for your third object with the last page missing. An Enid Blyton Toyland tales would be ideal or you could make up the script as shown below. Fourthly, have a calendar of the year, which is about to end and circle the 31st of December. It would be ideal to have the type of calendar where you pull off one day at a time. You may decide to print out from your computer- **December 31st** on a piece of paper and ask the children where they would expect to find what is printed on the card. Your fifth object is simply a card with the words **'THE END'** printed on it. With the exception of the first object you may want to put the others in a bag or case. Your last task is to look through your concordance and find Bible verses, which use the words **'THE END'**. They need to be understood by children as containing sad and glad uses of the phrase. Use three or more of these verses on a card or overhead projector. See below the verses I have selected from the N.I.V.

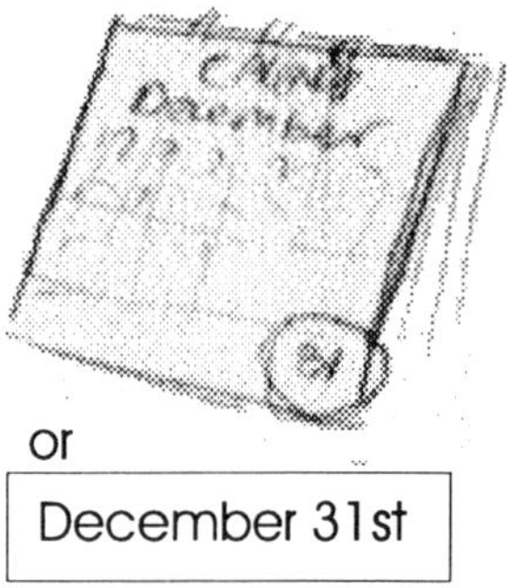

Well, Boys and girls, have you had a wonderful Christmas? Good! Today I have put this card on the board and I want you to imagine this is a cinema screen. Oh, I know the screens in a cinema are much bigger. I really want you to tell me how people usually know the film is finished. Can you tell me? (*You may get all sorts of answers here that are equally valid.*) Yes, that's the one I'm looking for. On the screen two words appear: "**The End**". (*Write the two words in felt tipped pen.*) Then come all the credits or long, long lists of the people who have acted in and helped to make the film. Now the end of a film can either make you sad or glad. Have you watched any sad films over the Christmas holidays? You can get some tearjerkers. You know the kind, everyone wants to wipe their eyes but doesn't want anyone else to see them do it, so they blow their nose instead which only makes more tears come. Then there are those other films, which end making you feel glad. The monster fell into the sea or evil people get locked away for life. Or these days they tend to get blown up at the end. So you can be sad or glad at the end of a film.

Let me dip into my bag for some thing else. What is this? (*Open up the wrapper and show the last bite of a chocolate biscuit.*) That's right, children, this is a piece of a chocolate biscuit. Can any clever child tell me which piece of the biscuit this is? Yes, it is the last piece. Have you any idea what sometimes happens to the last piece of a biscuit? It falls on the floor. You know there is nothing worse than losing the last piece. It's like losing the last piece of ice-lolly off the stick just as you take it up to your mouth. The last piece is so important. You know boys and girls; there are adults who are so busy talking as they eat that they forget they have eaten the last piece of their sandwich. Then someone near them puts their last piece down for a moment to go out, and when they return, their last piece has gone. They were looking forward to their last piece and then another member of the family says, "I'm sorry, but I thought I had one piece left to eat. I didn't realise I had eaten my whole sandwich." How would you feel if you lost your last bite of a chocolate biscuit or ice-lolly? Sad or glad? Yes, very sad indeed.

Let me dip into my bag again. What have I here? Yes, a book. This is an adventure book. Let me go to the end of the book and find out how the last story ends. (*You could make up your own ending such as: The toys had all been very sad knowing that one of them had stolen the Sugar Puffs. They heard little Mary coming. It was time to get back into the toy boxes but not before the patchwork doll told them who the thief was. "Do you know who the thief is, Patchy?" they asked sadly. "Yes, I do. The thief was someone who was up through the night and told us he was sleep walking, but the tell tale signs are all there, around the bowl. The guilty person was....*) Boys and girls the last page is missing. We don't know how it ends. If you had a book like that, how would you feel, sad or glad? Very sad. You would be rushing around to find out if a friend had the same book with the last page to find out who did it.

Let me dip into my bag once more. What might this be? Yes a calendar. Can you see which month it is? Yes, December. Can anyone spot the day? Yes, the 31st. You know children we have thought about, **the end of a film, the end of a biscuit, the end of a book.** Each one can make you sad or glad depending on what happens. But now we come to the end of a year. Here is what some verses in the Bible say about the end. See if you can tell me which make you sad or glad. (Put up your verses one after the other and ask which should make us glad or sad.)

1. For this God is our God forever and ever; He will be our guide even to THE END. Psalm 48v14.

2. There is a way that seems right to a man, but in THE END it leads to death. Proverbs 14v12.

3. Listen to advice and accept instruction and in THE END you will be wise. Proverbs 19v20.

4. And this gospel of the kingdom will be preached in the whole world as a testimony to all nations, and then THE END will come. Matthew 24v14. (*Explain here that some will be sad and others glad when the end comes.*)

5. And surely I am with you always to THE END of the age. Matthew 28v 20.

These are the promises from God's word the Bible, which can make the end of the year, glad. Through these promises we can look back with thankfulness and look forward full of wonder and praise for all that God can and will do for those who obey Him.

Oh, I have only one more thing to show you. (*Hold up a card with the words, "THE END".*) And I'm glad. Aren't you?

MOORLEY'S

We are growing publishers, adding several new titles to our list each year. We also undertake private publications and commissioned works.

Our range of publications includes:

Books of Verse:
- Devotional Poetry
- Recitations

Drama
- Bible Plays
- Sketches
- Nativity Plays
- Passiontide Plays
- Easter Plays
- Demonstrations

Resource Books
- Assembly Material
- Songs and Musicals
- Children's Addresses
- Prayers and Graces
- Daily Readings
- Books for Speakers

Activity Books
- Quizzes
- Puzzles
- Painting Books

Church Stationery
- Notice Books
- Cradle Rolls
- Hymn Board Numbers

Please send a stamped addressed envelope (approx. 9" x 6") for the current catalogue or consult your local Christian Bookshop who should stock or be able to order our titles.